Working Together for Local Integration of Migrants and Refugees in Amsterdam

This document, as well as any data and any map included herein, are without prejudice to the status of or sovereignty over any territory, to the delimitation of international frontiers and boundaries and to the name of any territory, city or area.

Please cite this publication as:
OECD (2018), *Working Together for Local Integration of Migrants and Refugees in Amsterdam*, OECD Publishing, Paris.
http://dx.doi.org/10.1787/9789264299726-en

ISBN 978-92-64-29971-9 (print)
ISBN 978-92-64-29972-6 (PDF)

Photo credits: Cover © Marianne Colombani

Foreword

An OECD-EU initiative: "A territorial approach to migrant integration: The role of local authorities"

This publication on *Migrant Integration in Amsterdam* was produced by the OECD as part of a larger study on "A Territorial approach to migrant integration: The role of local authorities" supported by the European Commission.

This study takes stock of the existing multi-level governance frameworks and policies for migrant and refugee integration at the local level in nine large European cities: Amsterdam, Athens, Barcelona, Berlin, Glasgow, Gothenburg, Paris, Rome and Vienna and a small city in Germany (Altena) thanks to the support of the German Ministry for Economic Affairs and Energy. It also builds on information collected from other 61 European cities, including Utrecht, through an ad-hoc survey and on a statistical database on migrant outcomes at regional (TL2) level. This study resulted in the **Working together for local integration of migrants and refugees Report**, approved by the OECD Committee for regional development policy (RDPC) in December 2017 (OECD, 2018 Forthcoming[1]).

The focus of this study is on ''migrants'', meaning a wide range of different groups of people with different reasons for leaving their countries of origin: humanitarian, economic, family or study, among others. The target group includes newcomers, from EU and non-EU countries, as well as migrants who settled in the cities many years ago and native-born with at least one migrant parent,[1] depending on the statistical definition used by the city. Given the recent increase in the arrival of refugees and asylum seekers to Europe, particular attention is paid to these groups throughout the case studies.

Cities in the sample have different track records in integrating migrants. The study looks at updates to the governance mechanisms in the wake of the recent influx of asylum seekers and refugees, in order to improve the local reception of migrants and the capacity to integrate them into the society. Conversely, it also investigates opportunities to extend some of the services recently established for newcomers to long-standing migrant groups.

The point of departure for the overall study is the observation that in practice integration takes place at the local level. Cities are focal spots of refugee and migrant reception and integration processes: in 2015, close to two-thirds of the foreign-born population in the OECD lived in urban areas (OECD, 2018 Forthcoming[1]).

The ambition of this series of case studies is to identify *how* cities have responded to these objectives. It aims to address an information vacuum: beyond the dominant literature on international and national evidence about migrant movements and integration, several studies exist about the local dimension and impact of migration.

---

1.   See definition of migration given below.

However, they do not explore the governance factor attached to it. In the view of partner cities and international organisations (UNHCR, etc.), multi-level governance can be an important explanatory factor of the performance of migrant integration policies. Even though migration policies are the responsibility of the national government, the concentration of migrants in cities, and particularly in metropolitan areas (Brezzi et al., 2016), has an impact on the local demand for work, housing, goods and services that local authorities have to manage. Local authorities act within a multi-level budgetary and administrative framework, which limits or adds responsibilities in dealing with migrant-specific impacts in their territory. As such, this work first aims at understanding the way cities and their partners address migrant integration issues. While it DOESN'T strive at this stage to evaluate the impact of the whole set of local public actions, it compiles qualitative evidence of city policies, decision making and evaluation processes across selected multi-level governance dimensions. These dimensions were selected according to the multi-level governance gaps analysis developed by the OECD (Charbit, 2011; Charbit and Michalun, 2009). Statistical data have been collected from all of the cities on the presence and outcomes of migrant and refugee populations.

As a result of this comparative work, and in collaboration with partner cities and organisations, the OECD compiled a list of key objectives to guide policy makers in integrating migrants with a multi-level perspective. The ***Checklist for public action to migrant integration at the local level, as included in the Synthesis Report*** (OECD, 2018 Forthcoming[1]) is articulated according to 4 blocks and 12 objectives. The four blocks cover: 1) institutional and financial settings; 2) time and proximity as keys for migrants and host communities to live together; 3) enabling conditions for policy formulation and implementation; and 4) sectoral policies related to integration: access to the labour market, housing, social welfare and health, and education.

This study first provides insight on the city's migration background and current situation. It then gives a description of the actions implemented following the framework of the "Checklist for public action to migrant integration at the local level".

The objective is to allow cities to learn from each other and to provide national and supranational decision makers and key partners of local integration policies with better evidence to address the major challenges ahead in this field and to adopt appropriate incentive schemes.

Acknowledgements

This publication on "Working together for local integration of migrants and refugees: The case of Amsterdam" was produced by the OECD in partnership with the European Commission as part of a larger study on "Territorial approach to migrant integration: The role of local authorities".

This case study has been written by Anna Piccinni, Policy analyst, under the supervision of Claire Charbit, Head of the Territorial Dialogue and Migration Unit, within the Centre for Entrepreneurship, SMEs, Local Development and Tourism of the OECD. This report is based on substantive inputs and contributions by Sjoerdje Charlotte Van Heerden (external consultant, University of Neuchatel), Lisanne Raderschall (OECD/CFE) and Paola Proietti (OECD).

The case study has been realised thanks to the close collaboration of the Municipality of Amsterdam who provided the information and organised the OECD field work. The Secretariat would like to express its gratitude to all the participants to the interviews (see Annex A). In particular to national government representatives and to the staff of the municipality: Jan van den Oord, Sabina Kekic and Idske de Jong for their continuous support throughout the realisation of the case study.

This case study benefitted from the comments of other colleagues across OECD directorates: Francesca Borgonovi (EDU), Thomas Liebig (ELS/IMD), Tamara Krawchenko (CFE), Annabel Mwangi (DCD).

The Secretariat is especially thankful for the financial contribution and the collaboration throughout the implementation of the project to the European Union Directorate General for Regional and Urban Policy. In particular we would like to thank Andor Urmos, Louise Bonneau and Judith Torokne-Rozsa for their guidance as well as for their substantive inputs during the revision of the case study.

Table of contents

Tables

Figures

Boxes

Abbreviations and acronyms

AZC	Asylum Seeker Centre (*Asielzoekerscentrum*)
COA	Central Agency for the Reception of Asylum Seekers (*Centraal Orgaan Asielopvang*)
GC	A Health Care Centre Asylum seekers (*Gezondheidscentrum Asielzoekers*)
GGD	Community Health Service (*Gemeentelijke Gezondheidsdienst*)
IND	Immigration and Naturalisation Service (*Immigratie en Naturalisatiedienst*)
MCA	Menzis COA Administration (*Menzis COA Administratie*)
RWITF	Refugee Work and Integration Task Force
RZA	Care Regulation for Asylum Seekers (*Regulering Zorg Asielzoekers*)
SZW	Ministry of Social Affairs and Employment.
UAF	University Assistance Fund (*Stichting voor Vluchtelingen-Studenten*)
UWV	Institute for Employee Benefit Schemes
VNG	The Association of Netherlands Municipalities (*Verenigde Nederlandse Gemeenten*)

Executive summary

This case study takes stock of the systems and policies in place to facilitate migrants and refugees integration in the city of Amsterdam. By situating local authorities in the existing multi-level governance framework this report sheds light on the resources and services made available to newcomers and longstanding migrants living in the city, emphasising which practices could inspire other cities elsewhere and which gaps still remain to be addressed. In particular, this report analyses Amsterdam response to the peak in refugees and asylum seekers arrivals since 2015 as an example for other cities due to its holistic approach and its time sensitiveness: starting providing very early measures after newcomers' arrival and sustaining them for the first three years.

A little more than half (51.66%) of Amsterdam's total population of 834 713 people, have a migration background, meaning are migrants themselves or native born with at least one migrant parent. Amsterdam affirms its cultural and ethnical diversity and pursues active policies to increase it by attracting international students and high-skilled migrants. The public opinion in Amsterdam has a positive perception of the measures undertaken since 2015 to welcome and integrate newcomers, as it emerges from the quarterly opinion polls that the municipality conducts since 2015. In the context of such high percentage of migrant population, the city doesn't implement group-targeted policies but aims at enabling all inhabitants to participate in the society and to have equal opportunities. In the absence of targeted measures, the city monitors the participation, opportunities and living conditions of different groups of citizens comparing their results by age, gender, level of education, immigrant background and residential neighborhood.[1]

As a thriving city, population is anticipated to increase by 23% up to just over a million in 2040, mostly due to internal and international migration, not last due to the recent influx of refugees.

Although Amsterdam is characterized by a high quality of life, and almost 90% of the population is satisfied with the city, delays and discrimination still penalises some migrants, in some cases also longstanding ones, questioning city's social cohesion. In view of future demographic growth these issues have to be analysed and addressed to avoid exacerbation. Unemployment and over-qualification gaps between "non-western migrants" (persons originating from a country in Africa, South America, Asia or Turkey) and their native-born and "western" counterparts are quite significant: the unemployment rate for the non-western migrant population (10.2%) is more than twice as high as that of the native-born population (4.7%). In terms of educational attainment, in 2016 50% of native-born and western migrants were highly educated, while only 26% of first generation non-western migrants and only 29% of the native born with at least one migrant parent reached higher education. In addition only about half of the population (49%) agrees that foreigners who live in their city are well integrated.

---

1.   See www.ois.amsterdam.nl/visualisatie/dashboard_diversiteit.html.

Historically, the integration model switched from group-specific policies (applied until 1990s) to universal measures, approximately in line with the national agenda for integration, focusing on problems that individuals face, rather than on their origin. However some measures remained specific to migrant groups such as the national policy on civic integration test (introduced in 2002) and language courses offer related to it as well as local initiatives to increase migrants participation and inter-ethnic contact among different groups. In 2016, the 'Amsterdam Approach' marks the city's further switch to a comprehensive group-specific policy package, to facilitate refugee integration, trying to avoid sequential provision of services and accelerating integration into the labour market.

Even though refugee arrivals over the last two years represent only 0.8% of the total migrant population, they acted as a **catalyst:** on the one hand revealing structural problems that persist in the city and are related to migration (i.e. availability of social housing, avoiding further social spatial segregation, school segregation, etc.). On the other these events pushed the city to experiment alternatives paths to avoid sometimes disappointing results of past integration trajectories, formulating a more connected, immediate and holistic approach. The Amsterdam approach, applied immediately after recognition combines language learning, health needs and path towards employment. The individual is valued for its competence and aspirations

The challenge ahead is to measure the effectiveness of this approach and, if proven successful, potentially extend it to different vulnerable groups. The holistic nature and systematic evaluation of the approach are unique characteristics that deserve being replicated elsewhere. This approach was made possible by the financial resources available (additional 2 million per year were allocated from the national level to refugee integration) and by the expertise that municipal staff had gain over years in questions related to migration and the strong relations with a network of non-state actors who could directly contribute to the response. This evolution makes Amsterdam an example of a local authority that is able to adapt and learn from the past 40 years of experience in integrating migrants.

Summary of key findings

1. Vertical co-ordination: Integration policies take place in a decentralised context, where local authorities often initiated integration policies as they had large competences in key sectors such as education and social policies. Even in those areas where the city is not directly in charge (i.e. language courses provision, etc.) it operates complementing national policies when needed. This is possible thanks to a general decentralisation tendency (i.e. Participatiewet 2015 and the housing legislation in 2014) and to the financial and implementation capacity of the city. There are risks and opportunities associated with the reallocation of competences. On the one hand, increased responsibilities imply challenges in terms of budget and information sharing across levels of government (i.e. data on registered asylum seekers/refugees). On the other it enables the city to directly design integration policies in closer consultation with the targeted groups (migrants and refugees) as well as to better evaluate the policies that have been locally formulated and implemented, thus integrating the results in the next decision-making cycle.

   The specificity of this model is not related to a specific degree of decentralisation but rather to its maturity and relationships among levels of government based on dialogue. The country has a strong tradition in national-local coordination, leaving the space to cities for engaging and putting forward local concerns. In this sense national and local policies on integration matters influence one-another without being necessarily aligned. The Association of Netherlands Municipalities (VNG) plays a unique role in channelling local level interest to the national level and brokers agreements on behalf of local governments on a variety of topics. Different levels of government as well as social partner dialogue through mechanisms such as the Refugee Work and Integration Task Force (RWITF).

With respect to the specific responses designed to asylum seekers and refugees arrivals since 2015, the central government on the one hand centralised the decision about dispersal policy on the other delegated some competences to the local level, such as housing responsibility through the "Asylum Influx Agreement" (2015). Most of the time the distribution of asylum seekers and refugees occurred in consultation with municipalities and the refugee centre in Amsterdam is a good example of how a municipality and the COA collectively co-ordinated and managed an effective and innovative shelter solution.

2. Cross-sectoral integration policy and co-ordination at city level: Informal and flexible mechanisms also characterise coordination around integration-relevant policies at the city level. Voluntary cooperation across departments largely depends on individuals and the political will shared by high-level decision makers. The city of Amsterdam has no overall integration strategy and there is no department specifically competent for migrant groups. In each policy sector, integration aspects have to be taken into account by the competent departmental service. With respect to the 'Amsterdam Approach' for refugee integration, horizontal cooperation across municipal departments is more regular and takes the form of a 'chain approach' involving all relevant staff in the implementation of the activities (i.e. Housing, Income, Work, Participation and Economics services etc.). From this informal approach the municipality is currently setting up a new Refugee department within the Work, participation and income department.

The informal approach to coordination with regard integration, except for refugee integration, has to be effectively monitored to ensure that all services directly operating with migrants simultaneously address different dimensions and obstacles to the process of settling in. The city could design a "road-map" approach that follows migrants from arrivals through the different turning points (i.e. integrating or re-integrating the job market, regularisation, housing, family reunification) they will face in their lives, identifying which entry points into the universal services could support migrants during these passages avoiding loopholes when moving from one legal status to another. In this sense the city could benefit from the examples of the Start Wien office or the Berlin Pass as cross-sectoral solutions that offer the most vulnerable categories integrated solutions to access services along their lives. With respect to departments' coordination around integration issues, the Integration and Diversity unit of the city of Vienna establishes contracts with all relevant departments to measure their achievements in terms of ensuring that migrants have equitable access to their services.

3. Proximity among city inhabitants of different origins: The city of Amsterdam adopted a definition of integration as a two-way process between host and newcomers. The key word is "connecting", *Verbinding*, emphasising how the municipality values activities and spaces for encouraging interaction among

different groups: native-born, long-standing migrant groups and newcomers. Best practices can be found in the (legal) space that the city provides for bottom-up initiatives, including the crowd-funded neighbourhood shelter Boost (see "Create spaces where the interaction brings migrant and native-born communities closer (Objectives 5)" in Chapter 4) that was set up by local volunteers for a small group of refugees and supported with a free venue donated by the municipality. The refugee centre established in the former prison is another example of connecting people. It provides space for over 70 local businesses and is an example of refugees interacting with the local business community and a way of working with the host community, since their arrival. In this respect, the city appears to recognise the added value of NGOs, associations and local initiatives in providing services for receiving and integrating migrants and refugees and is ready to exchange with national authorities to create the legal conditions for their action. Through these actors the city is best placed to create responses that fit the needs of newcomers and long-standing migrants alike, including those that are outside of its responsibility, such as language training. Similar approaches to host initiatives could be adopted by other Dutch municipalities and the national level could establish a way to incentivise cities to experiment with similar models. However, besides financial mechanisms, it is difficult to identify a stable entry point for NGOs and civil society to influence and be regularly involved in the city's migrant integration policy making and implementation. Contacts with foundations and key private sector players are punctual beyond the agreement with the 70 professional partners involved in the Refugee Talent Hub. As suggested by the Local Welcoming Policies for EU Mobile Citizens programme, the municipality should take the responsibility to create a platform that makes organisations and their activities visible, with the aim to stimulate co-operation and sharing of resources/experiences. In this sense the initiative of Paris to offer civil society organisation the opportunity to contribute to the formulation of the refugee integration strategy is remarkable.

4. Time and the need to accompany migrants throughout their lifetime: Learning from past experience, authorities are strongly focused on integrating newcomers right from the start. The city has implemented the Amsterdam Approach for refugees and asylum seekers, aiming at accelerating refugees' integration by focusing on the individual, through complementary measures towards employment, education and civic integration. Time is also crucial for migrants who are not refugees, as determined in the national policy obliging newcomers to take a civic integration exam within three years from obtaining their resident permit. Beyond the early days, the city must make services available and adaptable to the evolution of migrant situation over time. For instance, a specific need that will accompany a migrant during his/her entire life is access to health. The city should facilitate medical care for those who, after an initial phase, cannot obtain healthcare through regular and accessible routes due to persisting cultural and language barriers. For this reason the municipality can implement a set of measures that multiplies entry points over time for migrants to access services and connect with the local community, such as: accessible physical information points available in multiple languages, a user-friendly website, benefit from the experience of existing local communities, NGOs (i.e. GGZ Keizersgracht), small foundations in providing information and continuous support to migrants throughout their life, creating informal and formal information spaces where contacts can be fostered. Meevaart, the communal centre subsidised by the

municipality that is managed by residents of the neighbourhood – both national and migrants, including refugees – is a best practice. Such spaces that become an important part of the life of the community living in the area could be reproduced in other neighbourhoods or cities to improve cohesion and social linkages.

5. Capacity of the local authority to implement integration policies: There is no strong evidence that a policy strengthening skills and awareness is applied across the public function to ensure that migrants can easily access public services and can communicate in a language they understand. For instance, training for healthcare practitioners or teachers to recognise when something is wrong with new groups (human trafficking, abuse, etc.) could be strengthened. The city should systematically provide all civil servants with the correct information concerning regulations and laws (when are people eligible for healthcare/welfare benefits? When can they help a person who is not registered?). In the experience of the city of Vienna, which offers training since many years to municipal officers around integration issues, these efforts proved effective not only in increasing the capacities but also in helping the different departments why their contribution was important.

6. Evaluation: the Information, Research and Statistics Department of the municipality produces a number of reports (i.e. regular perception surveys, Jaarrapport integratie-Annual report on integration, evaluation of the Amsterdam Approach and the diversity monitoring) monitoring the results of different groups in Amsterdam. These monitoring contribute to ensuring that all citizens of Amsterdam are able to fully participate in society and could inform practices for data collection in other cities. However, strong mechanisms need to be in place to ensure that this information contributes to evidence-based policy making. Although most of the research is commissioned to the OIS by a policy department, it seems that mechanisms to ensure that policy makers use the results of the research to inform policies could be strengthened. In addition in such a complex political sector many dimensions should be considered when assessing the impact of a integration policy (i.e. assessing the impact of suppressing allocation to national migrant associations in terms of introduction of newcomers to their new destination culture, avoiding isolation and exclusion experiences; etc.). To better assess the measures undertaken the perception of all communities need to be taken into account, as well as indicators of migrants' contribution to social, cultural and economic city's development beyond traditional outcomes indicators (educational attainment, inclusion in the labour market, etc.). The Score card and current surveys are good examples that need to be sustained and could be completed by participatory assessments. The specific data collection and cost-effectiveness (MKBA) evaluation of the Amsterdam Approach Status holders is a very innovative monitoring system to measure the efficiency and effectiveness of this policy and the results will be essential for shaping future integration policies.

7. Integration in the labour market: Amsterdam has a strong vocation for attracting skilled migrants and has set up centres – such as the IN Amsterdam-International Newcomers Amsterdam – to facilitate their arrival and settling in the city. A formal agreement with companies exists within the Refugee Talent Hub and the municipality also sets an example by hiring refugees. However, access to the job market seems to be often penalised by the absence of social capital and discrimination as demonstrated by persistent gaps across generations of migrants although educational qualifications for children with migrant parents from non-

western backgrounds tend to increase. The city might consider increasing sensitization mechanisms to change employers mentalities and make it attractive for business to hire migrant and refugees, as the city of Berlin has done through public communication campaigns. The city could communicate to migrants and refugees more targeted information on their labour rights and mechanisms to detect abuse. In addition it could be considered if some of the measures currently experimented for refugees (i.e. early capacity screening, matching mechanisms, coaching initiatives, etc.) could be valuable for migrants in general. For example, it is not clear what follow up has been given to the Letter and Action Plan signed in 2015 between the municipality and relevant labour market players (confederation of industries, employment agency, etc.) advocating for strong collaboration and matching mechanisms to strengthen the employability of refugees. A more permanent task force or roundtable including municipality, entrepreneurs, employment agency and migrant associations could give continuity to these engagements, filling gaps in understanding what role the private sector could have in fostering migrant and refugee integration and what contribution these groups could make to their businesses.

8. Long and short term measures to increase housing availability and reduce city segregation

Increasing housing prices as well as a growing population are likely to aggravate currently moderate spatial segregation and make it difficult for many residents to afford living in the city centre. Ethnic concentration in deprived neighbourhoods might become more accentuated outside of the administrative perimeter of the city and the relation between migrant localisation and well-being inside the entire metropolitan area should be better understood. Currently, registration time for social housing stands at 8.7 years (2015). To meet housing needs of refugees the municipality is providing them priority access to social housing through an exemplary mechanism of collaboration has been put in place between the housing associations, the municipality and the province. To avoid further spatial segregation, housing corporations allocate refugees, entitled to a unit, in all parts of the city. More on the long term, city efforts to increase affordable housing for all groups, include introducing income based social housing rent increases to incentivise higher middle income individual to free-up space for lower income residents. Further to avoid segregation, creative urban policies aim making housing available in the short term by transforming underused or unused spaces into mixed and heterogeneous neighbourhoods, while 30% of all new housing stock is designated to vulnerable groups (including refugees). Interesting peer learning could be done with the city of Gothenburg, which is implementing a housing development plan with similar ambitions.

9. Equalising access to quality education across the schools

In some of Amsterdam's schools the student population does not represent the diversity of the neighbourhood and in schools with higher concentration of migrant pupils, students tend to have lower performance, with potential consequences on their access to the job market. Since the 1990s the city aims at balancing migrant pupils' distribution across schools. It does so by trying to influence the parental choice and concentrating investments in schools with weak performance indicators. Currently, schools in Amsterdam receive funding for every refugee student enrolled. Students have been distributed across 114 schools to avoid a concentration of newcomers in specific neighbourhoods and increase the budget of as many schools as possible. It would be interesting to closely monitor the results of this dispersion in terms of educational attainment, after-school social inclusion and professional inclusion.

Key data on migrant presence and integration in Amsterdam

Figure 0.1. Amsterdam's geographic location in the Netherlands according to the OECD regional classification

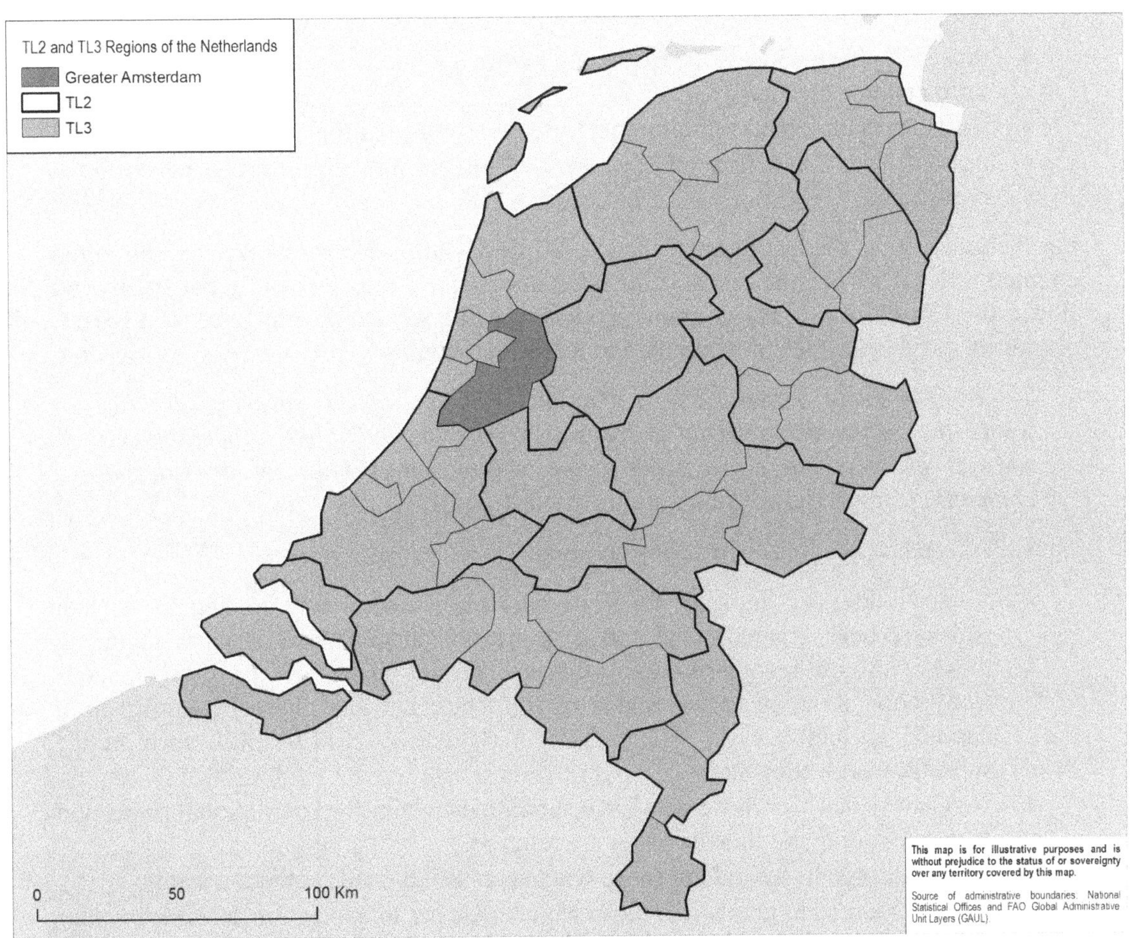

Source: OECD (2018), OECD Regional Statistics (database), http://dx.doi.org/10.1787/region-data-en.

Municipality	TL3	TL2	State
Amsterdam	Groot-Amsterdam Greater Amsterdam	Noord-Holland	Netherlands

Note:
TL2: Territorial Level 2 consists of the OECD classification of regions within each member country. There are 335 regions classified at this level across 35 member countries
TL3: Territorial Level 3 consists of the lower level of classification and is composed of 1681 small regions. In most of the cases they correspond to administrative regions.

This section presents key definitions and a selection of indicators about migrants presence and results in Amsterdam.

Definition of migrant and refugee

The term 'migrant' generally functions as an umbrella term used to describe people that move to another country with the intention of staying for a significant period of time. According to the United Nations (UN), a long-term migrant is "a person who moves to a country other than that of his or her usual residence for a period of at least a year (12 months)". Yet, not all migrants move for the same reasons, have the same needs or come under the same laws.

This report considers migrants as a large group that includes:

- those who have emigrated to an EU country from another EU country ('EU migrants')
- those who have come to an EU country from a non-EU country ('non-EU born or third-country national')
- native-born children of immigrants (often referred to as the 'second generation')
- persons who have fled their country of origin and are seeking international protection.

For the latter, some distinctions are needed. While asylum seekers and refugees are often counted as a subset of migrants and included in official estimates of migrant stocks and flows, the UN definition of 'migrant' is clear that the term does not refer to refugees, displaced, or others forced or compelled to leave their homes:

The term 'migrant' in Article 1.1 (a) should be understood as covering all cases where the decision to migrate is taken freely by the individual concerned, for reasons of 'personal convenience' and without intervention of an external compelling factor. (IOM Constitution Article 1.1 (a)).

Thus, in this report the following terms are used:

- 'Status holder' or 'refugee' for those who have successfully applied for asylum and have been granted some sort of protection in their host country, including those who are recognised as 'refugees' on the basis of the 1951 Geneva Convection Relating to the Status of Refugees, but also those benefiting from national asylum laws or EU legislation (Directive 2011/95/EU), such as the subsidiary protection status.
- 'Asylum seeker' for those who have submitted a claim for international protection but are awaiting the final decision are referred.
- 'Rejected asylum seeker' for those who have been denied protection status.
- 'Undocumented migrants' for those who decide not to appeal the decision on their asylum seeker status or do not apply for another form of legal permission to stay.

This report systematically distinguishes which group is targeted by policies and services put in place by the city. Where statistics provided by the cities included refugees in the migrant stocks and flows, it will be indicated accordingly.

Source: OECD (2016), *International Migration Outlook 2016*, OECD Publishing, Paris, http://dx.doi.org/10.1787/migr_outlook-2016-en; UNSD (2017), "International migration statistics", United Nations Statistics Division, https://unstats.un.org/unsd/demographic/sconcerns/migration/migrmethods.htm#B.

In contrast to other countries, statistics on the immigrant population in the Netherlands are often not based on nationality but ethnicity, distinguishing between *allochtonen* and *autochtronen*. The terms stem from the Greek term *autochtron* meaning "native". *Allochtonen* are referred to if at least one parent was born outside the Netherlands. Netherlands Statistics (CBS) is aware of the social debate around it the terms allochtoon and autochtron, and introduced in its Annual Report 2016 a new terminology: persons with a Dutch or migrant background.

In this case study, we adopt the statistical categories of the Dutch system. A person with a Migrant background is defined as a person of whom at least one parent was born abroad, this includes "second-generation migrants" or "native-born with at least one migrant parent" (HWWI, 2007[2]). Within this category a distinction is possible between persons with a "western" migration background and persons with a "non-western" migration background. Person originating from a country in Africa, South America or Asia (excl. Indonesia and Japan) or from Turkey are defined as "non-western" migrants.

Key statistics

All the below statistics refer to 2016 (unless stated differently). Numbers and percentages were provided by the city of Amsterdam unless stated otherwise. See Jaarboek Amsterdam (2016), *Amsterdam in cijfers 2016* for the most comprehensive overview.

1. Presence of population

1.1 Country subnational government expenditure as a per cent of GDP: 30.1% (OECD average = 40%)

1.2 Total city population in January 2016: 834 713

1.3 Population with a migration background in Amsterdam in 2016:

Including first-generation migrants (foreign born) and second-generation migrants (native born with at least one migrant parent): **51.66% of the total population** or 431 237 inhabitants, of which:

1.3.1

First-generation migrants	29.3%
Second-generation migrants	22.4%
Non-migrants	48.3%
Total	≈ 100%

1.3.2

Non-western migrants	34.8%
EU migrants	10.1%
Other western immigrants	8.7%
Non-migrants	48.3%
Total	≈ 100%

*1.4 The most important countries of origin of the migrant population, 2016:**

Morocco   17.4%

Suriname   15.3%

Turkey   9.9%

Indonesia   6.0%

Germany   4.2%

* Share of the migrant population.

There has been an increase of 41% of mobile EU citizens since 2004. The largest number of arrivals over the past two years are: United States (3 014), India (2 560), United Kingdom (2 586), Germany (2 418), Italy (2 390) and France (2 072).

1.5 Irregular migrants: the city does not have any official statistics.

1.6 Number of refugees/status holders, 2016:

In 2015 the number of refugees and asylum seekers to Amsterdam increased by 38% compared to previous years.

In 2016 there were 3 412 refugees in Amsterdam, representing 0.8% of the total migrant population. 38% of these refugees are considered "recently" arrived (in the preceding two years), another 34% settled in the city less than five years ago. There were approximately 200 asylum seekers.

2. Employment

2.1 The main industrial sectors where migrants work:

1. Wholesale and retail trade, repair of motor vehicles and motorcycles, transportation and storage, accommodation and food service activities

2. Information and communication; financial and insurance activities; real estate activities; professional, scientific and technical activities; administrative and support service activities

3. Human health and social work activities

2.2 Per cent in paid employment[1] of Amsterdam population aged 15-74, 2015:

Non-western migrants   57.1 %

Western migrants   70.0 %

Non-migrants   70.2 %

2.3 Per cent unemployed[2] of Amsterdam population, 2012-16:

	2012	2013	2014	2015	2016
Non-western migrants	12.8%	14.4%	14.5%	12.4%	10.2%
Western migrants	5.4%	7.4%	6.4%	7.2%	6.1%
Native born	4.6%	5.9%	5.7%	5%	4.7%
Total population	7.3%	8.9%	8.5%	7.6%	6.7%

2.4 National Dutch statistics for unemployment, 2016 (CBS, 2017[3])

Native born 4.9%

Western migrants 8.6% (2015)

First-generation non-western migrant background 12.5%

Second-generation non-western migrant background 14.3 %

Total population 6%

3. Education

3.1 Educational attainment for population groups in Amsterdam aged 15-74 years old in 2013:

Lower education includes primary education, intermediate preparatory vocational education or level 1 of secondary vocational education. *Intermediate education* is secondary vocational education, senior general secondary education or pre-university education. *Higher education* englobes higher vocational education or academic education.

	Lower education	Intermediate education	Higher education	
First-generation migrants	41%	33%	26%	≈100%
Second-generation migrant	30%	40%	29%	≈100%
Non-migrants	17%	33%	50%	≈100%
Surinamese	41%	43%	16%	≈100%
Antilleans	33%	43%	24%	≈100%
Turks	57%	32%	11%	≈100%
Moroccans	57%	33%	10%	≈100%
Other non-western migrants	39%	35%	27%	≈100%
Western migrants	17%	34%	49%	≈100%
Non-migrants	17%	33%	50 %	≈100%

3.2 Level of education for refugees, 2011-14:

Without elementary education	16%
No elementary education or elementary education not completed	20%
Completed secondary education	19%
Completed intermediate vocational education	5%
Completed higher vocational education	10%
Hold a master degree	3%

Source: Gemeente Amsterdam (2015).

4. Income

4.1 Average annual personal income in Amsterdam, 2013

Non-western migrants	EUR 24 600
Western migrants	EUR 39 300
Non-migrants	EUR 37 200

*4.2 Net annual household income for migrant population in Amsterdam, 2015**

EUR 0-20 000:	39%
EUR 20 000-40 000:	41%
EUR 40 000-60 000:	13%
EUR 60 000-80 000 :	4%
> EUR 80 000:	3%

* Wage earner is of migrant origin.

*4.3 Recipients of social benefits in Amsterdam by immigrant background and gender, 2017**

	Men	Women	
Non-western migrants	51%	49%	≈ 100%
Western migrants	47%	53%	≈ 100%
Non-migrants	54%	46%	≈ 100%
Unknown	64%	36%	≈ 100%

* N = 39 978.

5. Political participation

Right to vote: Active and passive (to vote and to run for office) voting rights follow after naturalisation (newcomers have to pass the Civic Integration exam - *Wet Inburgering Nieuwkomers*- within three years of receiving their legal residence permit in order to be naturalised. Once the exam is passed, and within five years of receiving their residence permit, they can be naturalised). All voters have to be 18 years and older.

5.1 % of Amsterdam's population with a migration background has the right to vote during general elections in 2017:

	First-generation	Second-generation	Total
Non-western migrants	72%	98.8%	80%
Western migrants	24.1%	97.5%	48.5%

The threshold for voting in local elections is lower as since 1985 non-EU citizens have the right to vote if they have at least five years of legal residency in the Netherlands. This results in higher voter turnout of immigrants compared to other European countries and allows considerable levels of political representation in the City Council (de Graauw and Vermeulen, 2016).

5.2 % of non-western migrant-origin voters in Amsterdam, 2014 (Kranendonk et al., 2014).

Morocco	24%
Suriname	26%
Tukey	34%
Overall turnout in municipality	51%

6. Housing

6.1 Key figures for the housing sector (total population):

Housing stock of Amsterdam, January 2016:

Owner-occupied 29.5%

Rental social housing (corporation owned) 44.5%

Private rental 25.9%

Average net rental costs for social housing in Amsterdam (2015): EUR 496

Average net rental costs for private rentals in Amsterdam (2015): EUR 745

Notes

1. At least one hour paid employment per week.

2. Unemployment rates here follow the definition of the International Labour Organisation (ILO): the share of people aged 15-74 years old in the total labour force who are not in paid employment or self-employment, who have been seeking work recently and who are currently available to work.

Introduction

The objective of this case study is to provide an analysis of refugee and migrant reception and integration policy in Amsterdam. The study highlights the design and implementation of integration actions within the Dutch multi-level governance framework for migrant integration, as well as interactions between the municipality and other public and non-state stakeholders. The study is based on answers to a questionnaire from the municipality of Amsterdam and its partners (January 2017), interviews conducted with different stakeholders (see Annex A for a complete list) involved in integration during an OECD mission (21-23 February 2017), and existing data and literature. A first version of this case study was finalised in June 2017 and updated in December 2017.

The city of Amsterdam has historically been a city of immigration and plays a proactive role in migrant integration. The conceptual approach to migration and integration followed similar trajectories at the national and city levels, while objectives have not always been aligned. The Netherlands is a pioneer among EU countries; Sweden, which started integration policies in the mid-1970s, is the only EU country that launched integration policies before the Netherlands. The Netherlands introduced a co-ordinated approach to migrant integration, at both the local and national level, in the early 1980s. During the 1960s and 1970s, newcomers were seen as "guest workers" in a multicultural society, who would eventually return to their countries of origin (Bruquetas-Callejo et al., 2007). During the late 1970s and early 1980s, the city of Amsterdam adopted a pluralist minorities policy, supporting the integration of minorities while maintaining their cultural identity and establishing dedicated dialogues with each community. Special attention was given to empowering ethnic communities in their bridging role for newcomers into a new society (Hoekstra, 2014; de Graauw and Vermeulen, 2016; Butter, 2009).

Since the 1990s, however, this model has been slowly abandoned, both at the national and more gradually at the local level, and more proactive measures were introduced to counter the disadvantaged socio-economic position of migrants that had become increasingly apparent. In the late 1990s, a Diversity Policy was established that involved a frame-shift from a 'group-specific policy' to 'problem-oriented policies' (Scholten, 2014[4]). Claiming that cultural and religious matter belonged to the private realm, cultural and religious groups were no longer object of specific measures in favour of a generic, individual oriented approach. In addition area-based integration polices were adopted at the local level in particular in the four largest Dutch cities (including Amsterdam), in order to deal with complex socio-economic problems like segregation, poor housing, poverty and unemployment all of these cities faced (Tersteeg, A.K., R. van Kempen & G.S. Bolt, 2013). Further the creation of a special minister for Integration and Large cities at the national level signifies a period of increased coordination in policy making and tendencies to decentralise the issue of integration in the 1990 (Scholten, 2014[4]). The concept of voluntary integration was first emphasised in 1994 in the Integration Policy, which insisted on the need for migrants to learn Dutch; it was institutionalised in 2007 by the introduction of the compulsory civic integration exam - *Wet Inburgering Nieuwkomers* - that newcomers have to pass within three years of receiving their legal residence permit in order to be naturalised. Once the exam is passed, and within five years of receiving their residence permit, they can be naturalised.

Overall, the city's approach shifted from group-specific to problem-oriented policies (Maussen, 2009). In 2003, the city passed an act to end policies targeting groups on the basis of their nationality and ethnicity and pushed for mainstreaming migrant integration into all sectors of the city's policies. Since then the municipality affirms its active role in designing the integration process operating in the interstices of universal sectoral policies, sometimes above and beyond its administrative responsibilities, to address the needs of its migrant population as one among other groups who live in the city.

In the wake of the increased arrival of refugees to the city in 2015, the municipality responded to the needs of newcomers with strong leadership and using all the margin for manoeuvre available within its flexible national-local co-ordination and funding mechanisms. This study thus devotes particular attention to the multi-level governance of Amsterdam's response to integration and reception of newcomers, and in particular to the "Amsterdam Approach". In collaboration with national authorities and civil society organisations, Amsterdam took the opportunity to integrate lessons learnt from the past in the formulation of this new approach. The "Amsterdam Approach Status holders"[1] specifically targets refugee reception and integration by creating opportunities for participation and inclusion right from the start, building bridges with the local population and other long-term migrants. With its tailored support to enter an education or labour path, the Amsterdam Approach Status holders represents an exception to the generic need-based approach to service provision for migrants that the municipality adopted since late 1990s. Yet, it also exemplifies a prototype allowing the city to experiment with more comprehensive service provision, which could be extended and adjusted to different groups based on their needs, once proven successful.

The study is structured as follows. Part One, offers a snapshot of Amsterdam's migration today, including stock, historic migrant and refugee flows and nationalities, key laws, and the main issues emerging in the city related to migrant integration. Part Two presents the city's institutions relevant for integration and responses to the reception and integration of migrants and refugees. These responses are presented according to the objectives identified in the OECD's "Checklist for public action to migrant integration at the local level" (OECD, forthcoming[5]). The first block of the Checklist presents the multi-level governance setting that applies to Amsterdam's integration policy; the institutional mapping helps clarifying the allocation of competences across levels of government. The second block describes how integration solutions are conceived in a continuum over time and aim at creating proximity and participation from all groups. The third block overviews operational, capacity building and monitoring tools used by the city for implementation. The last block introduces sectoral actions to facilitate integration through labour market, education, housing and social services.

Notes

1.   See https://amsterdamsmartcity.com/projects/the-amsterdam-approach-to-asylum-statusholders.

Part I. Migration snapshot of the city of Amsterdam

Chapter 1. Migration insights: Flows, stock and nationalities

For centuries Amsterdam has been a city of immigrants. It currently hosts 180 different nationalities and 51.7% of its population has a migration background[1] (OECD Questionnaire, Amsterdam, 2017). First-generation migrants who live in Amsterdam represent 29.3% of the city's population.

The history of migration in Amsterdam can be broken down into different phases. In the 1960s Amsterdam attracted predominantly migrants from the former Dutch colonies, particularly Suriname and Indonesia, as well as guest workers from the Mediterranean countries, notably Morocco and Turkey (de Graauw and Vermeulen, 2016). Today these groups make up 48.6% of the total migrant population (both first- and second-generation). In the 1980s, new arrivals came from ex-Yugoslavian countries, followed by new EU-accession countries in the 2000s. These phases of migration were accompanied by different conceptual frameworks and policies for integration.

Free movement within the EU and the European Free Trade Association resulted in a rise of migrant inflows in the Netherlands, from 19 000 in 2003 to 65 000 in 2013. In 2013, only 9% of the total permanent migration inflow was composed of non-EU nationals, which corresponded to 0.04% of the population in the Netherlands (OECD, 2017a) while in 2015 half (81 000 EU citizens moved to the Netherlands in 2015) of new immigrants to the Netherlands were EU citizens (OECD, 2017a). Over the past few decades the Netherlands has also attracted a large international student population, supported by the offer of university degrees taught in English (OECD, 2016a). The Netherlands granted 15 200 residence permits to international students in 2015, representing 9% of the student population in the country (OECD, 2017a). About 20% of the students who graduate in Amsterdam remain there afterwards (Amsterdam Municipality). Amsterdam is further developing specific integration policies addressing EU migrants, including the growing population of "EU mobile citizens" who work for international businesses and are based in the city for shorter periods of time.

Like in many other European cities, the number of refugees and asylum seekers to Amsterdam increased by 38% in 2015 compared to previous years. In 2016, the city housed approximately 3 412 refugees and asylum seekers, mostly from the Syrian Arab Republic, Ethiopia and Eritrea. They represent 0.8% of the total migrant population in Amsterdam. In 2015, the Netherlands received 43 000 asylum seekers (EUROSTAT, 2016a) the equivalent of 3% of the applications received in the EU28. Asylum applications to the Netherlands were 44 000 in 2000 (CBS, 2001)[2]. In addition, 800 refugees benefitted from the resettlement programme in 2014 (UNHCR, n.d.). In 2015, 3 900 unaccompanied minors filed asylum requests in the Netherlands, which is four times the number of requests received in 2014 (OECD, 2017a).

Around 4.7% of all refugees recognised in the Netherlands are allocated to Amsterdam; in 2016, Amsterdam was the first municipality in terms of absolute number of asylum seekers hosted in reception centres, while also being the most populated municipality in the Netherlands (data from the municipality of Amsterdam). The city anticipated the arrival of more refugees for 2016 and prepared adequate solutions for the temporary accommodation for these newcomers (see "Secure access to adequate housing (Objective 10)" in Chapter 6). Although fewer refugees arrived in Amsterdam than expected in 2016, these structures have been established and the city is prepared in the event of a future increase in arrivals.

Figure 1.1. Total asylum applications in the Netherlands

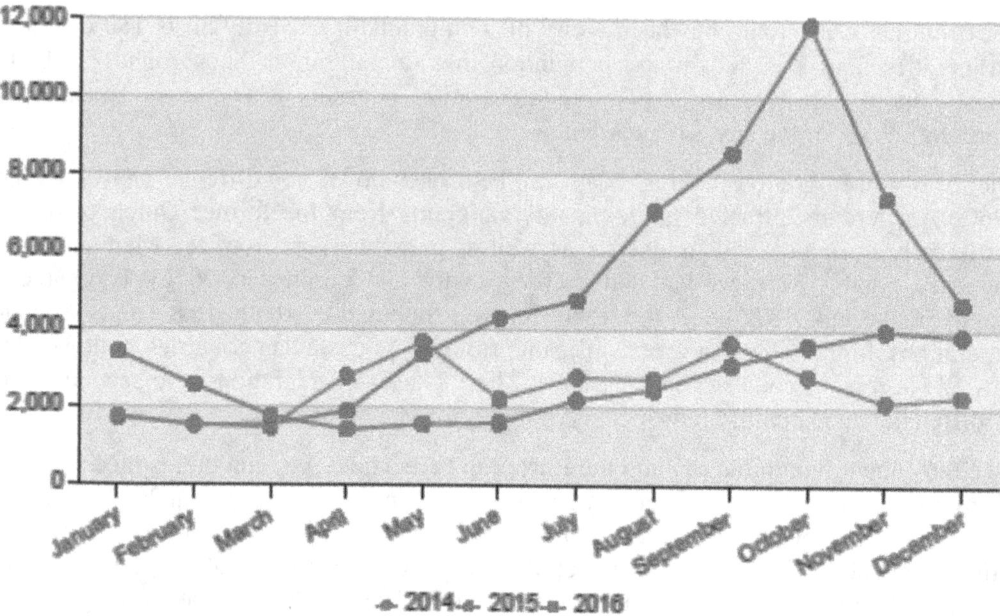

Source: Dutch Ministry of Security and Justice.

Notes

1.   This percentage includes second-generation migrants, born in the Netherlands from at least one foreign-born parent.

2.   See   www.cbs.nl/en-gb/news/2002/04/slightly-more-asylumseekers-in-eu-strong-fall-in-the-netherlands.

Chapter 2. City well-being and inclusion[1]

The following sections will introduce some integration outcomes while describing residential and social segregation issues that characterise the city of Amsterdam.

Out of the almost 400 municipalities in the Netherlands, Amsterdam is the most populous one (the seat of the Dutch government is in The Hague). In the province of North Holland (TL2) where Amsterdam is situated, well-being is similar to the country average, which is high in comparison to the OECD average (OECD, 2016a).[2]

Figure 2.1. Well-being in North Holland and the national average, 2016

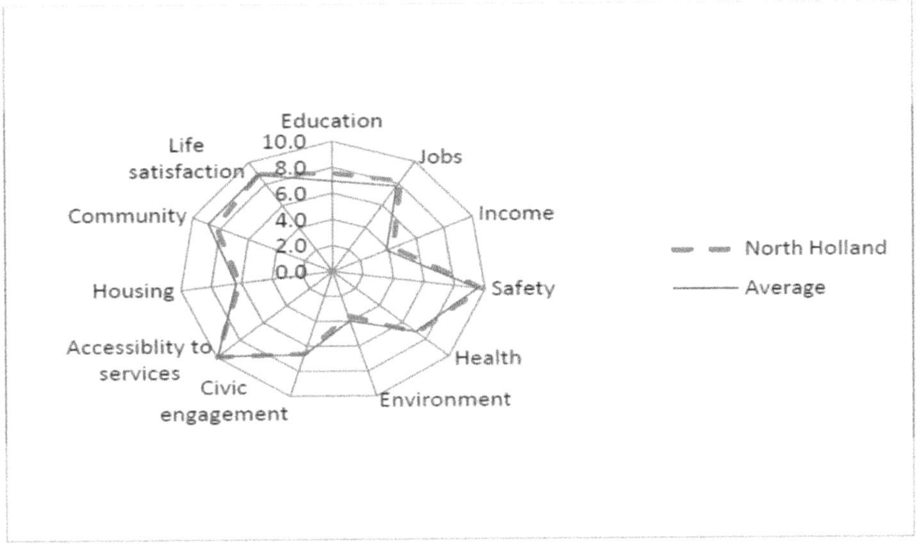

Source: OECD (2016e), OECD Regional Well-Being.

Well-being data for the region of North Holland indicate that it performs particularly well compared to the national average on access to services, safety, life satisfaction and community. On the contrary, indicators related to housing, income and environment are weak compared to the rest of the country (OECD, 2016e).

Amsterdam is the centre of population growth in the Netherlands. According to OECD estimates (OECD, 2017g) the city's population will increase by 23% between 2017 and 2040, while in Greater Amsterdam the population will increase by 20% and in the Netherlands only by 6%.

In 2013, the poverty rate in Amsterdam stood at 18.2%: this was surpassed only by Rotterdam, at 18.7% (Statistics Netherlands, 2015). In Amsterdam, like in many metropolitan areas in the OECD, while the average income and purchasing power are above the national average, there are large differences across the city, often also expressed by gaps in educational outcomes (OECD, 2016g). Similar to many large cities, there is a risk that the poorer districts overlap with areas largely populated by ethnic minorities, thus creating disadvantaged neighbourhoods with high concentrations of low-income groups and high levels of social and ethnic inequalities (OECD, 2006). In these neighbourhoods, segregation processes might be accelerated because residents who can tend to leave predominantly low-income neighbourhoods. Some areas in the centre of Amsterdam are characterised by incomes well above the national average; however, in such districts as Geuzenveld-Slotermeer, Bos en Lommer and Zuidoost, nearly 25% of households live below the "social minimum" (Gemeente Amsterdam, 2015). These districts have a high concentration of people originating from Suriname, Turkey and Morocco (Cities for Local Integration Policy Network, 2010).

Figure 2.2. Share of inhabitants of non-western origin, Amsterdam, 2016

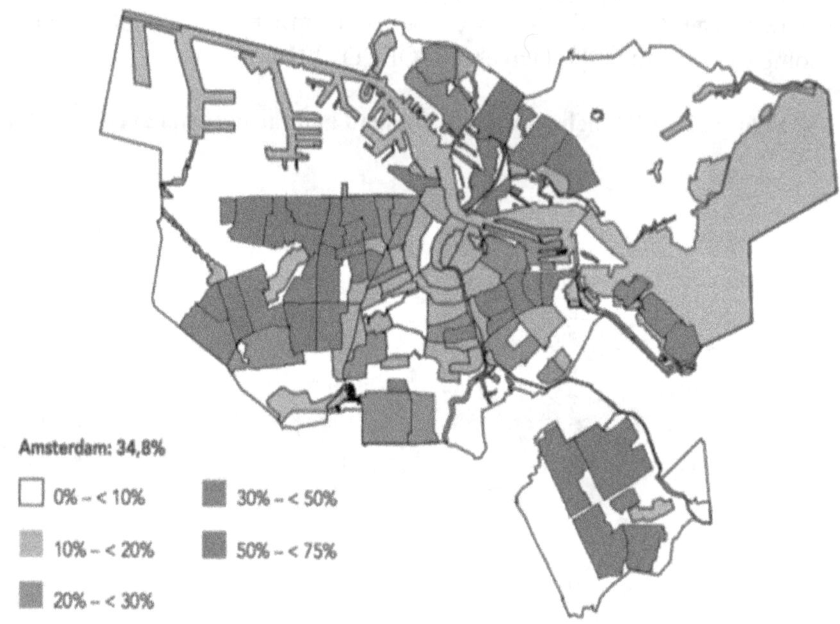

Source: OIS. Jaarboek Amsterdam (2016), *Amsterdam in cijfers 2016.*

Despite these differences, according to the terminology used by municipal officers, Amsterdam is generally described as moderately segregated compared to other cities of the same size. In fact, among the cities with the highest proportion of low-income residents in the Netherlands, Amsterdam has the lowest degree of spatial segregation – low-income residents are relatively evenly dispersed among the city's neighbourhoods (OECD, 2017g).

Economic integration and employment

Table 2.1 shows that both native Dutch and migrants living in the region of North Holland (TL2) have higher employment and participation rates and lower unemployment rates than the national average. North Holland is characterised by a demand of labour. However, the unemployment rate in Amsterdam in 2016 (6.7%) was slightly higher than the national average (6%) (see Indicators 2.3, 2.4 in Key statistics above).

Table 2.1. Labour sectors for native and foreign-born workers, North Holland and the TL2 average, 2014-15

North Holland and the TL2 average, 2014-15

	Native born			Foreign born		
	Employment rate	Unemployment rate	Participation rate	Employment rate	Unemployment rate	Participation rate
North Holland	77%	6%	82%	65%	10%	72%
National average	75%	7%	80%	61%	13%	70%

Source: OECD database on migrant population outcome at TL2 level.

The distribution of native and foreign workers across sectors in North Holland is almost identical for both categories of people.

Table 2.2. Labour sectors for native and foreign-born workers, North Holland and the TL2 average, 2014-15

	Native-born			Foreign-born		
	Agriculture	Industry	Services	Agriculture	Industry	Services
North Holland	2%	12%	87%	1%	12%	87%
National average	3%	17%	80%	2%	20%	79%

Source: OECD database on migrant population outcome at TL2 level.

As indicated in the city key data above (see Indicators 4.1 and 4.2), in 2013 the average annual income of non-western immigrants in Amsterdam was EUR 12 600 (34%), lower than that of the non-migrant population. In 2015, more than 40% of the population with a migrant origin in Amsterdam earned between EUR 20 000 and EUR 40 000 per household annually while the national gross household disposable income in 2013 was USD 29 185 (or EUR 24 363 current prices) (www.OECD.Stat.org).

Non-western immigrants were the most affected by the economic crisis. However, since 2014 unemployment rates for all migrant, and in particular non-western ones, have tended to decrease (Statistics Netherlands, 2016). Difficulties entering the job market seem to remain across generations for people with a non-western background. In fact, at the national level, despite better basic educational qualifications (MBO level 2 or more, HAVO or VWO), the Dutch-born non-western background population has a higher unemployment rate (14.3%) than first-generation migrants with a non-western background (12.5%) and is much higher than for the native born (4.9%) (Statistics Netherlands, 2017). Unemployment is higher for the youngest cohort (15-25 years old) with a non-western background (22% in 2015) compared with 9% for Dutch-born and 15% of western migrants in the same age cohort. This difference has been increasing since 2008 (Statistics Netherlands, 2016). Between 2012 and 2016, 10.2% of non-western migrants in Amsterdam were unemployed whereas only 4.7% of non-migrants and 6% of western migrants were unemployed (*cf.* Key data at the beginning of the case). Difficulties in accessing the labour market can also be distinguished for specific nationalities. According to the migration association Euro-Mediterrean Centrum Migratie and Ontwikkeling (EMCEMO), 40% of the working-age Dutch population with a Moroccan origin is unemployed (interview 17 May 2017).

Housing

According to a social segregation index, which represents the percentage of low-income households that should move to achieve a completely equal distribution, the city has a moderate level of spatial segregation (Statistics Netherlands, 2014). Amsterdam scores lower on this index than all other major cities in the Netherlands. Further, according to a study comparing the situation in 2001 to that in 2011 for 13 European cities, Amsterdam is the city in which the social mixing of population groups has shown a slight increase (Tammaru et al., 2016; Hoekstra, 2014). The large social housing stock, which in 2015 stood at over 50% of the total housing stock, and its ubiquity and active policies for urban renewal have contributed to producing mixed and heterogeneous neighbourhoods. For instance, since the onset of the crisis, only a few middle-class families in Amsterdam have moved out of inexpensive social housing units, thus maintaining the level of diversity (Tammaru et al., 2016). Still, most social housing is concentrated on the outskirts of the city, with much fewer social housing in the centre and south district (OECD, 2017g). The peripheral districts show a high concentration of people originating from Suriname, Turkey and Morocco, leaving these non-western migrants spatially separated from their more affluent counterparts or native-born Amsterdammers (Cities for Local Integration Policy Network, 2010) There is a risk for "suburbanisation of poverty" (OECD, 2017g), as the inner city is less accessible and affordable and the share of social housing is diminishing. Moreover, as the price of houses within the A10 ring motorway, which delimits the city centre, rises there is a risk of polarisation, as only low-wage earners through social housing and high-wage earners who can pay high private market rent will be able to live there, leaving out middle-income earners (OECD, 2017g).

The accessibility to social housing for lower wage earners became a concern in the late 1990s when the government privatised the housing sector, which lead to rent increases and a decrease in the available social housing: the average registration time for social housing increased to 8.7 years in 2015, compared to 7.9 years in 2010 (Jaarboek Amsterdam, 2016). Under such circumstances, providing affordable housing for all groups and avoiding further segregation is a challenging task for the municipality.

Some segregation is evident between Dutch and migrant cohorts (Musterd and Van Gent, 2016). According to the municipality, many of today's challenges result from an approach that perceived immigration as a temporary phenomenon requiring minimal policies and guidance. Housing problems first arose in the early 1980s when most of the housing for foreign employees was closed due to bad housing conditions. As a result, more migrants started to enter the social housing market, leading to concentrations of (especially people originating from Turkey and Morocco) migrants in the most deprived neighbourhoods. During this period, the city of Amsterdam became more aware of its status as a city of immigration and the related social implications in terms of segregation and discrimination this entailed. Initiatives started to foster integration, including new housing projects, mostly through individual rent subsidies based on income and household composition. These projects managed, to a certain extent, to improve living conditions, but mainly appeared insufficient because of the large influx of new migrants. A differentiation in housing prices within neighbourhoods was not achieved and today the high rental prices near amenities reflect this trend. As a consequence, a higher concentration of economically disadvantaged people, among them many ethnic minorities, lived together in less-developed neighbourhoods where rents remained lower.

Education

The patterns of uneven distribution among housing and employment for non-western migrants and their children mirrors to a certain extent their representation in schools as well as their educational attainment. In the region of North Holland, the foreign-born population generally lags behind the native-born population in educational performance. While 41% of the native-born population is highly educated, only 30% of the foreign-born population reaches this level.

Table 2.3. Educational attainment for native-born and foreign-born population, North Holland and the TL2 average, 2014-15

	Native born			Foreign born		
	Low educated	Medium educated	Highly educated	Low educated	Medium educated	Highly educated
North Holland	20%	39%	41%	30%	40%	30%
National average	25%	44%	32%	32%	45%	23%

Source: OECD database on migrant population outcome at TL2 level, forthcoming.

The divide is even greater in Amsterdam: roughly 50% of the non-migrant population in 2013 were highly educated against nearly 30% of second-generation migrants and 26% of first-generation migrants (see Data 3.1 in the City migration identity card). In particular, non-western migrants – predominantly those with a Turkish or Moroccan background – have on average a lower level of educational attainment than their western migrant counterparts (OECD questionnaire filled by the Municipality of Amsterdam, 2017). Generally, however, educational levels have been increasing for all groups in Amsterdam (Hoekstra, 2014). Over the last ten years, the number of non-western or western background university students has doubled compared to the rates of the native population (Hoekstra, 2014).

In Amsterdam, as well as in other large cities, educational inequality and lack of opportunities for social advancement are framed within the debate on school segregation (Tammaru et al., 2016). This debate has been present in Amsterdam since the 1990s and refers to the diverse ethnic composition of students in the schools across the city, with over 60% concentration of migrant-background students in some schools, often those associated with poor performance (de Graauw and Vermeulen, 2016). The debate points to parents' choice of their children's school as a very highly valued principle that could have slowly contributed to increasing levels of school segregation (OECD, 2010b) as many non-migrant families choose to place their children in schools with fewer migrant students. As a consequence, the student population often does not represent the diversity of the neighbourhood around the school (Hamilton, 2015; Arts and Nabha, n.d.). It has proven difficult to combat segregation and concentration in schools and according to some studies (Arts and Nabha, n.d.) in the Netherlands there are approximately 500 schools with a majority of students with a migration background. Demonstrations against the closure of two of these schools took place in 2015 in Amsterdam.

As education is a key element of overall integration, a more balanced distribution is needed and quality education needs to be accessible for all, especially considering the newly arrived refugees that will further diversify the population. With regard to the educational level of refugees who arrived in the Netherlands in 2015, estimations from the Central Agency for the Reception of Asylum Seekers (COA) suggest that about one-third have a higher education. The COA further indicates that refugees residing in Amsterdam are somewhat less educated than national average: approximately 15% are highly educated, 40% have an intermediate education, and 45% is not or has a lower educational attainment (Germeente Amsterdam, 2015).

Box 2.1. Key observations

- Amsterdam has a long history of immigration. Today 51% of its population has a migration background.
- The city presents a moderate level of segregation compared to other cities of the same size.
- Population growth induced by migration and the high number of tourists led to an increase in prices on the private rental market making, especially the inner city became less accessible and affordable.
- Efforts to counter school segregation have been in place since the 1990s and should continue in order to ensure more equal access to quality education and to reduce the gap in educational attainment between non-migrant background population and the other groups.
- There is high labour demand in Amsterdam and North Holland which can be filled thanks to migration flows. However obstacles in accessing the labour market seem to persist across generations of migrants and have to be further analysed and addressed.

Notes

1. Unless stated differently, all information in this paragraph has been gathered from municipal authorities through OECD research.

2. Please see the interactive graphics available at: www.oecdregionalwellbeing.org/region.html#NL32.

Part II. Objectives for effectively integrating migrants and refugees at the local level

This section is structured following the Checklist for public action to migrant integration at the local level, as included in the Synthesis Report (OECD, 2018 Forthcoming [2]) which comprises a list of 12 key evidence-based objectives, that can be used by policy makers and practitioners in the development and implementation of migrant integration programmes, at local, regional, national and international levels. This Checklist highlights for the first time common messages and cross-cutting lessons learnt around policy frameworks, institutions, and mechanisms that feature in policies for migrant and refugee integration.

This innovative tool has been elaborated by the OECD as part of the larger study on "Working Together for Local Integration of Migrants and Refugees" supported by the European Commission, Directorate General for regional and urban policies. The Checklist is articulated according to four blocks and 12 objectives. Part 2 gives a description of the actions implemented in Amsterdam following this framework.

A checklist for public action to migrant integration at the local level

Block 1. Multi-level governance: Institutional and financial settings

Objective 1. Enhance effectiveness of migrant integration policy through improved vertical co-ordination and implementation at the relevant scale.

Objective 2. Seek policy coherence in addressing the multi-dimensional needs of, and opportunities for, migrants at the local level.

Objective 3. Ensure access to, and effective use of, financial resources that are adapted to local responsibilities for migrant integration.

Block 2. Time and space: Keys for migrants and host communities to live together

Objective 4. Design integration policies that take time into account throughout migrants' lifetimes and evolution of residency status.

Objective 5. Create spaces where the interaction brings migrant and native-born communities closer

Block 3. Local capacity for policy formulation and implementation

Objective 6. Build capacity and diversity in civil service, with a view to ensure access to mainstream services for migrants and newcomers

Objective 7. Strengthen co-operation with non-state stakeholders, including through transparent and effective contracts.

Objective 8. Intensify the assessment of integration results for migrants and host communities and their use for evidence-based policies.

Block 4. Sectoral policies related to integration

Objective 9. Match migrant skills with economic and job opportunities.

Objective 10. Secure access to adequate housing.

Objective 11. Provide social welfare measures that are aligned with migrant inclusion.

Objective 12. Establish education responses to address segregation and provide equitable paths to professional growth.

Chapter 3. Block 1. Multi-level governance: Institutional and financial settings

Enhance effectiveness of migrant integration policy through vertical coordination and implementation at the relevant scale (Objective 1)

Division of competences across levels of government

The Netherlands is a decentralised unitary state (OECD, 2017c). The subnational level comprises two tiers of government with general competencies: the provinces (*provincies*) and the municipalities (*gemeenten*). Each level of government has its own responsibilities, with the national government providing unity through legislation and supervision (OECD/UCLG, 2016). The municipality of Amsterdam is located in the province of North Holland. In the Dutch territorial governance system, the central and local levels of government are generally the strongest, with the provincial level in between, with relatively less power. For example, provincial budgets are only about one-tenth of the municipal budgets (OECD, 2017f). However, the provinces play a key role in vertical co-ordination, bringing together formal and informal stakeholders from the different levels of government.

Figure 3.1. Levels of governance in the Netherlands

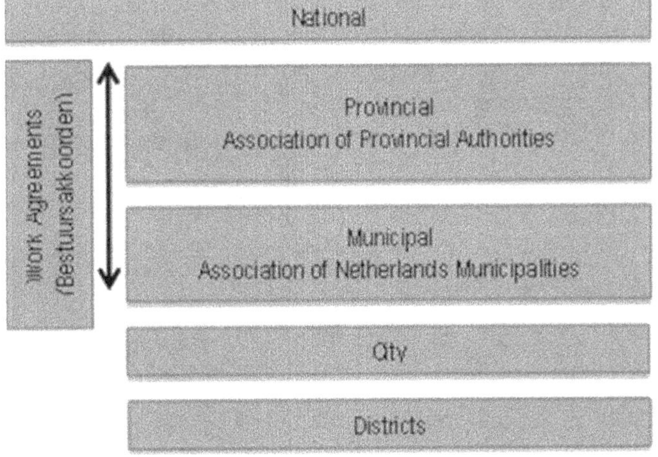

The Dutch system has evolved over recent years as a result of continuous decentralisation processes. The central government is generally responsible for tasks concerning the Dutch society as a whole. It also provides general guidelines for future development and operates directly at the local and regional levels through a large number of central government agencies, directly controlled and financed by the central government, such as the regional labour market offices, regional police services or regional healthcare services (OECD, 2014). The centrepiece of the co-operation between the subnational and central levels are several work agreements (*bestuursakkoorden*) on a wide variety of topics (Charbit and Romano, 2017[6]). Associations of local governments such as the Association of Netherlands Municipalities (Vereniging van Nederlandse Gemeenten, VNG[1]), the Association of Provincial Authorities (Inter-Provinciaal Overleg, IPO) and the Association of Regional Water Authorities (Unie van Waterschappen, UvW) (OECD, 2014; 2010) are involved in these agreements. In particular, the VNG takes part in every decision were municipalities are involved: housing, employment, health, civic integration, participation, etc. The VNG is the main negotiator with the government. These work agreements grant the provincial and municipal levels a relatively large degree of autonomy. While they lack legislative powers, these levels can make additional regulations within the framework of national regulations.

The municipal government is seen as the main provider of public services to the citizens. In particular, the municipal level is responsible for: the establishment and maintenance of primary and secondary education institutions as well as oversight of the implementation of the national education act, adult and vocational education programming and funding, elderly and child care, youth policy, health (general health services, healthcare for drug addicts, centres for homeless people), local social assistance (immigrant reception, employment and income services), local measures for participation and access to the labour market, urban planning, planning permission, participation in housing association decisions with regards to social housing and building on municipal land, municipal medical and administrative services, public order and safety, public transport, the environment, the harbour and many other services.

The city of Amsterdam is further divided into seven geographical city districts. City districts were created in the 1980s and until 2014 had an elected committee (*bestuurscommissie*). They presently carry out the tasks delegated by the municipal council. City districts usually have five or six departments covering general affairs/governance (public services, logistics, personnel, post and communication services); finances; public space and the environment; well-being (social work, nurseries, elderly and youth, immigrants); education (primary schools) and sports; and labour and housing (markets, shops, building permits, land use). Districts are also responsible for garbage collection, green spaces and the provision of district-bounded welfare services, but they may also support and facilitate migrant integration programmes.

Allocation of competences for specific migration-related matters (excluding status holders)

Figure 3.2. Institutional mapping of the multi-level governance of integration related policy sectors

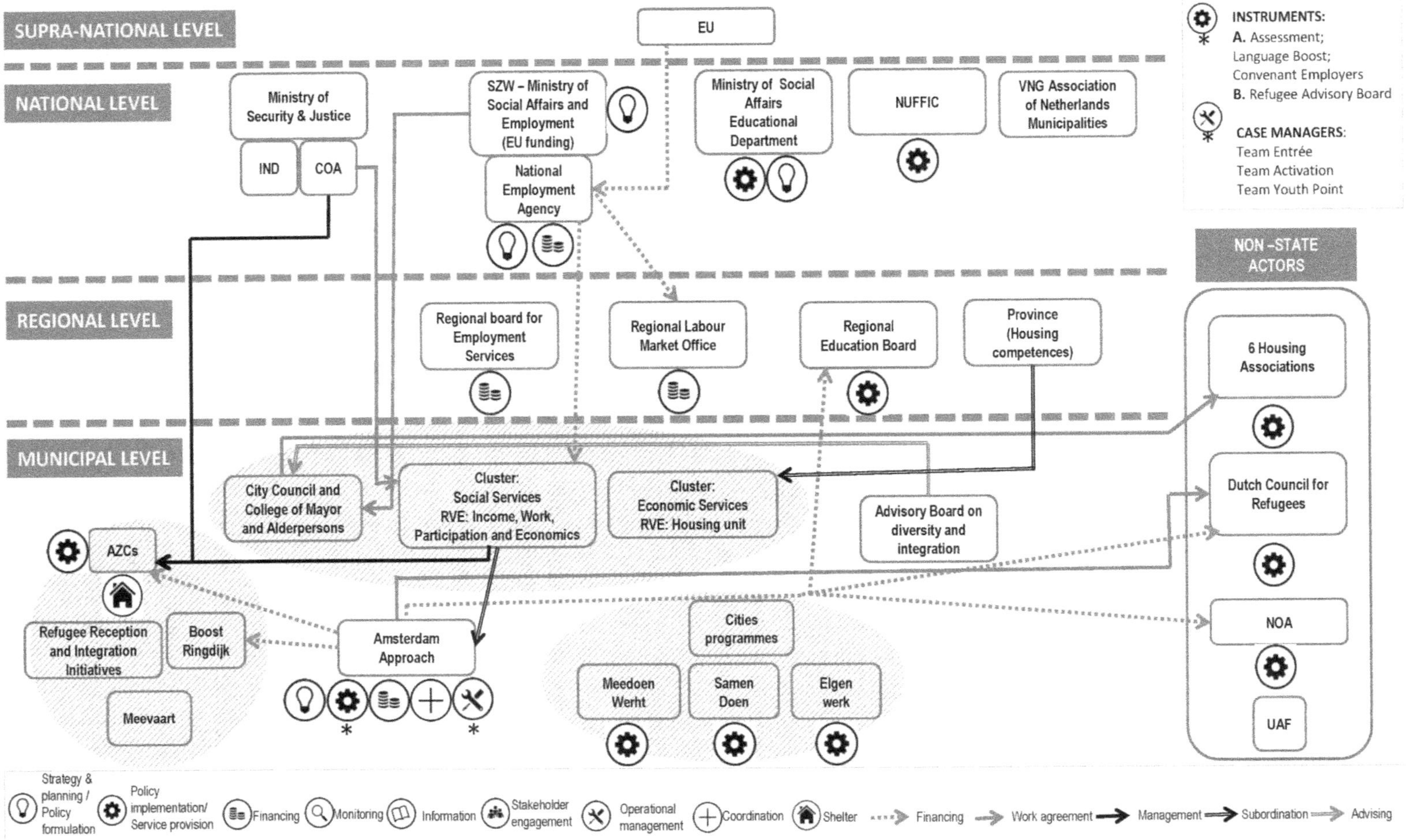

Source: Author's own elaboration.

With regards to migrant integration, Annex B summarises the division of tasks across the three levels of government for some key competences. It is worth highlighting that until a change in the law in 2013, one specific competence of the municipality in integration matters was to provide language courses (with components on healthcare, childcare and work integration) to migrants who have to pass the Civic integration exam. For this purpose, a specific municipal department had been set up (Education and Integration). Since 2013 this competence is now attached to the national Ministry of Social Affairs and Employment, which organises courses to pass the civic integration exam[2] and provides third-country nationals with a loan of EUR 10 000 to cover the costs of language training along with an additional EUR 350[3] to enrol for the exam. Since this change, the city of Amsterdam only offers language courses to people who do not fall under the Civic Integration Law.[4]

Integration-related national-local co-ordination mechanisms

The Dutch government has not adopted a national integration strategy, beside the organisation of the Civic Integration exam, and doesn't monitor the progress of local authorities against it. National authorities do not dispose of legislative or fiscal means to regulate some of the competences related to migrant and refugee integration. Therefore, they use incentives and have developed alternative measures for co-ordination and dialogue. The central level influences integration results by applying incentives on key groups. For instance the Ministry of Social Affairs and Employment (SZW) offers wage-cost subsidies (i.e. offering a fiscal incentive to a company for hiring students as a trainee) to enterprises to make it profitable to employ certain categories of personnel, for instance migrants and refugees.

In terms of co-ordination mechanisms, there is a tradition in Dutch politics of consensus-based decision-making processes, in dialogue among policy levels, allowing the local level, as well as social partners to engage and voice their position. Recently this practice was applied to issues related to the increase in refugee and asylum seekers arrivals (see Box 3.1) making communication more fluid. As a result, contrary to the other case study cities, stakeholders in Amsterdam did not experience an information gap with the central level. An example of multi-level dialogue is the issue-based roundtables recently organised by the SZW bringing together national and local stakeholders. These dialogue mechanisms provide a space to discuss also migrant and integration-related topics and to adopt nation-wide measures. For instance, the issue of discrimination was addressed with trade unions and the chamber of commerce, as well as representatives from the VNG, launching a programme to raise employers' awareness of discrimination and introducing anonymous job applications. Another thematic discussion addressed youth involvement to stimulate integration. This practice is in line with traditional Dutch political decision-making model, the so-called "polder model" of achieving deliberation through bargaining between government, trade unions and employers unions.

Further, a new National Action Programme to combat discrimination was announced in January 2016 and is being implemented across all levels of government and encompasses an increased focus on the prevention and awareness of discrimination as well as greater institutional capability to deal with cases of discrimination (OECD, 2017a).

Another example of national/local co-ordination mechanisms related to migration policy is the regional health co-ordinator that has been established by the national Ministry of Health with competences for each working area of the community health services (see Objective 11 for more information).

Box 3.1. The Refugee Work and Integration Task Force (RWITF)

At the national level, a Refugee Work and Integration Task Force (RWITF) was established to co-ordinate work among the key actors involved in the reception and integration of asylum seekers. This umbrella organisation brings its stakeholders together regularly. The most directly involved national ministries and actors are: Social Affairs and Employment; Security and Justice; Education, Culture and Science; the Central Agency for the Reception of Asylum Seekers (COA); and the Institute for Employee Benefit Schemes (Uitvoeringsinstituut Werknemersverzekeringen, UWV). The municipalities are represented through the Association of Netherlands Municipalities (Vereniging van Nederlandse Gemeenten, VNG) and the G4 composed of the bigger Dutch cities of Amsterdam, Utrecht, Rotterdam and The Hague, as well as the Social and Economic Council. In addition, social partners and key non-governmental organisations are involved, for example the Dutch Council for Refugees (Vluchtelingenwerk), the University Assistance Fund (Stichting voor Vluchtelingen-Studenten, UAF), Dutch refugee organisations and Divosa (association of executives in the social domain). A website* provides information about legislation, policy, support options and best practices for employers, educational institutions and social organisations (Ministry of Social Affairs and Employment, 2016). This constitutes an example of unique vertical co-ordination that also serves as a platform for engaging non-state actors and produces critical information for all actors involved in the response to refugee reception and integration.

* www.werkwijzervluchelingen.nl.

Interaction with neighbouring communes to reach effective scale in social infrastructure and service delivery to migrants and refugees

As mentioned above, the VNG is the municipalities' main negotiator with the central government when it comes to aligning national objectives for migrant integration with local ones (concerning housing, employment, health, civic integration, etc.). Co-ordination between different cities, including the city of Amsterdam, and other municipalities is clearly institutionalised through the VNG. Amsterdam is closely tied to the VNG, and the Alderperson, who is responsible for the portfolio's work, participation, income of Amsterdam, is currently a member of the VNG board, and is chairing the VNG Commission of Work and Income. This allows for high-level representation in the VNG and also links the two institutions through one person.

The city of Amsterdam co-ordinates with municipalities and provinces across its functional urban area through the Amsterdam Metropolitan Area (Metropoolregio Amsterdam, MRA). Established in December 2007, this informal partnership makes agreements in the fields of traffic and transport, economy, urbanisation, landscape and sustainability; it has a revolving presidency among its member municipalities and provinces. Three committees drive its work: 1) planning; 2) accessibility/transportation; and 3) the economy. Some of its tasks include: jointly agree and co-ordinate on housing issues; transform offices into temporary spaces for living and working through such measures as flexible zoning; transform and/or restructure the obsolete greenhouse area at Greenport Aalsmeer into new spaces for living and/or working (OECD, 2017g).

In addition, Amsterdam is member of a union composed by three other major Dutch cities, the so-called: G4 (composed by the city of Amsterdam, The Hague, Rotterdam and Utrecht). The G4 was established in the 1990s and since 2003 is also represented in Brussels, where it monitors EU policy and legislative developments. Based on the initiative of the G4, a Large Cities Policy (GSB) was established in the Netherlands allowing cities to determine for themselves how results shall be achieved in different areas. Between 2005 and 2009, "improving integration and citizenship" was one of the main topics of the GSB, which includes 31 large and medium-sized cities (European Urban Knowledge Network, 2012). Over the course of this period, 38 more medium-sized municipalities formed a similar network, referred to as the G32. Together the G32 and the G4 form the G41. The goal of this network is to represent the common interests of the cities to other levels of government and to exchange knowledge, including on migration and integration policies when relevant.

In May 2016, the 35 municipalities, including Amsterdam, which make up the Labour Market Regions, applied for a European Social Fund (ESF) of EUR 116 million targeting refugee integration. The programme aims at helping status holders find jobs and learn the language. Through this co-operation, additional finances were made available to municipal authorities (Ministry of Social Affairs and Employment, 2016). The municipalities of this region co-operate and have regular meetings involving representatives of the private sector to mobilise the largest employers of the region's 35 municipalities.

Seek policy coherence in addressing the multi-dimensional needs of, and opportunities for, migrants at the local level. (Objective 2)

City vision and approach to integration

As elaborated in part one of this case study, large gaps can be observed with regards to educational and labour indictors comparing Amsterdam's native-background and migrant-background populations. Further, recent surveys show that 28% of the non-western residents in Amsterdam feel discriminated against (Geemente Amsterdam, 2016a) and only about half of the population (49%) agrees that foreigners who live in their city are well integrated (EUROSTAT, 2016b). This data indicates the need for an even higher level of engagement from the city's leadership to further improve integration outcomes and the perception of different groups.

While there is no migrant integration strategy as such, the city has formulated in its policy documents a definition of integration as "mutual acceptance by both the host society and immigrants, as well as active participation by the immigrants" (Gemeente Amsterdam, 2003) which includes a socio-cultural focus compared to policies in other cities or at the national level that are more focused on socio-economic aspects of integration (Scholten, 2012). The city's approach values the contribution that migrant bring to the society by, as a municipal administrator said during OECD fieldwork, "building an urban network around migrant and refugees".

Box 3.2. Evolutions of integration concepts and regulations at national and local level

Great changes occurred regarding the vision and policy of integration, which has occupied a central place in Amsterdam's social and political life since the 1970s. It can be said, that local and national integration policies largely followed the same trajectory regarding changes made in integration policy (Scholten, 2012). When the country received the first large waves of immigrants, who were predominantly from Morocco and Turkey, in the 1960s and 1970s, they were called "guest workers", under the assumption that they would eventually return to their home countries. Multiculturalism as each ethnic minority maintaining their identity and culture of origin was then the main approach at national and local level (Bruquetas-Callejo et al., 2007). In the late 1970s and early 1980s, the city of Amsterdam pushed further the national view of multiculturalism and adopted a pluralist minorities policy: minorities should integrate while maintaining their cultural identity. However, once it appeared that the nature of the migrants' stay was not temporary, their disadvantaged socio-economic position increasingly became a topic of concern. Municipalities were the first to get involved in providing housing, education, healthcare and welfare for migrants, pressuring the national authorities to recognise and finance these measures. In parallel since the 1980, local and national level slowly shifted away from the vision of a multicultural society, towards more proactive approach to learning the language and integrating. The 1994 integration policy for ethnic minorities (Contourennota Integratiebeleid Etnische Minderheden) emphasised the need for migrants to learn Dutch and Dutch culture.

In addition to self-responsibility, the narrative of integration policies moved towards a need-based "generic" approach in the attempt to achieve universal access to services for all individuals. Integration is about targeting individual's situation of vulnerability and talent (Bruquetas-Callejo et al., 2007) rather than groups, through policies that are "generic where possible, and specifically where necessary" (Wittebrood and Andriessen, 2014: 5). In this sense, in 2003 a note was published in Amsterdam aiming at reducing the specific character of integration policy and mainstreaming it into general policies. Thus, policy is not determined for pre-defined groups, but if it appears that certain characteristics (e.g. age, origin, level of education, sexual preference) are strongly correlated to specific problems, policy can be tailored towards these aspects. As an example, specific compulsory integration courses are offered to migrants. In 2005 the city issued a memorandum called "We the people of Amsterdam", emphasising the link between integration, participation and interethnic contact and also pursuing harder measures regarding crime and radicalisation (Scholten, 2012).

More recently in 2007, the Dutch government introduced a compulsory civic integration exam for third-country nationals (Wet Inburgering Nieuwkomers), emphasising the voluntary aspect of integration. Newcomers have to pass a language and culture test within three years of receiving their legal residence permit in order to be naturalised. Once the exam is passed, and within five years of receiving their residence permit, they can be naturalised. A new provision was added in October 2017: the participation declaration adhering to Dutch norms and values, illustrating the perception of integration as a necessary step on the side of the migrant who needs to show his/her willingness to adhere to national rights and obligations.

The current policy vision is implemented through: 1) a close monitoring of socio-economic results of all groups in the city in order to identify potential obstacles to equal services and opportunities (see "Monitoring integration outcomes" in Chapter 5); and 2) the development of transversal thematic strategies and policies. These initiatives address certain factors that could have an impact on the outcomes of specific groups including migrants. These thematic strategies are implemented across the municipal departments and in collaboration with civil society. Examples of thematic strategies that the city developed to raise awareness around cultural diversity and to act upon factors undermining integration are: Amsterdam Human Rights Agenda – aiming at creating a just living environment for all through knowledge of the rights-; the "Sharing History" programme -to teach residents about the history of their city and inhabitants-; the city Policy Framework Anti-discrimination (2015-19) and the Implementation Pink Agenda (LGBTQI empowerment), such as racism, discrimination, radicalisation, etc.

More recently the city created entry points for specific migrant groups who seek opportunities to become active citizens, get engaged in the city, understand and share its values. While breaking the generic approach, these measures embrace a voluntary vision of integration, where individuals are enabled to build their own diverse urban network. The city identified some groups, who are left out of the national Civic integration policy, who felt their language skills were not sufficient to fully integrate into Dutch society and cultural life. Thus the municipality extended language and cultural courses to EU migrants, over 65 and migrants who already passed the civic exam. Comparably, the "Local Welcome Policies for EU Mobile Citizens" is a one-stop-shop for EU migrants who want to better integrate and participate in the city life. The city's practices targeting EU citizens are shared with other European cities and resulted in a "Welcome Europe toolkit: Local welcoming policies for EU citizens".[5]

Lately municipal policies included group-targeted measures to respond to the increase in refugees and asylum seekers arrivals. The "Amsterdam Approach Status-holders", that will be explained in detail in "The Amsterdam Approach Status-holders: Time applied to refugee integration" in Chapter 4, is in line with the idea of building a network around newcomers and tailor educational or employment opportunities to the person's capacities and aspirations. Whether this policy is to be understood as another flection from traditional generic approach or whether, based on the results of the current experience, the municipality will lean towards more group-specific measures is something to be decided when designing the next local policies based on the results of the ongoing evaluation.

Communication with citizens

The city affirms its cultural and ethnical diversity and pursues active policies to increase it by attracting international students and high-skilled migrants. However it doesn't produce communication campaign around integration issues, probably because it would be hardly relevant to communicate about such a vast and diversified group that represents 51% of the population. Nevertheless several efforts have been put in place since 2015 to communicate the city's response for receiving and integrating refugees and to measure the opinion of the public by conducting quarterly surveys on the perception to the measures displayed to welcome refugees.

In particular the city communicated around the decision to give priority access for refugees to social housing (see Objective 10). Only 14% of the respondents to a survey conducted by the city (see "Intensify the assessment of integration results for migrants and host communities and their use for evidence-based policies (Objective 8)" in

Chapter 5) is in favour of this regulation, while 86% of the respondents support the housing of refugees in vacant office spaces, buildings or churches (Gemeente Amsterdam, 2016b). To avoid tensions with host communities over this decision, the municipality set up four locations for dialogue to explain clearly the rule of the distribution of housing.

Horizontal co-ordination infrastructure at the city level

In the city, powers are divided between the deliberative council (*gemeenteraad*, also referred to as the municipal or City Council) elected by popular vote, and the executive body called the College of Mayor and Alderpersons (*college van burgemeester en wethouders*) appointed by the City Council, except for the Mayor. Following the 2014 City Council elections, a governing majority was formed between the social liberal party D66, the conservative-liberal party VVD and the socialist party SP. This is the first coalition without the social-democratic labour party PvdA since the Second World War. At time of writing the city had nine alderpersons, all with a different portfolio and responsibility for a district. For instance: aldersperson for "Employment, income and community participation", for "Education, youth, diversity, integration and the City district of East", etc. Under the city council and College of Mayor and Alderpersons, four main clusters make up the city's administration: economic services, community services, administrative services and social services (see Figure 3.2). These clusters include multiple departments (RVEs) that fit within the specific domain but have their own expertise. Departments can work together on certain policies, within and between clusters.

While the next section discusses the governance of the refugee reception and integration programmes in more details, here we focus on the interactions of the different departments involved in delivering services relevant for integration issues. There is no stand-alone unit dealing with migrant integration. In the past there were some units, such as the Education and Citizenship (Educate en Inburgering) Unit or the Diversity Unit (Unit Diversiteit), which were directly in charge of providing citizenship and language courses for immigrants and of the implementation of the policies towards immigrant associations, as well as the Platform Amsterdam Together (PAS), which ran a programme "We Amsterdammers" from 2005 to 2010. The organigram changed as a consequence of the 2013 reform which centralised the competence for providing language and cultural courses to migrants from the municipal to the national government.

Portfolios often do not overlap between political and administrative levels. For instance, an alderperson in charge of employment, income and community participation is responsible for issues that cut across the social services as well as the economic services of the city's administration. At the same time these same departments could also partially be under the political responsibility of other Alderperson in charge for instance of youth. Thus a transversal issue, such as integration, not only falls within the responsibility of different departments but also of different decision makers. To what extent this plays in favour of more coherent integration policies depends on many factors. For instance, this could translate in a lack of strong leadership, as responsibility is shared across different alderpersons. On the other hand, a common political will shared by several high-level decision makers can make integration the priority in the work of all departments.

An example of a horizontal mechanism for sharing responsibilities across city departments for policies related to migration issues is the anti-discrimination policy. Several administrative portfolios are concerned by this cross-cutting issue: public order and safety, education, work and economy, and municipal personnel management. Beyond the city's administration, other partners are involved in the implementation of this strategy, including the Amsterdam Discrimination Complaints Office, the Amsterdam police unit, the Public Prosecution Service, civil society organisations and city districts (Gemeente Amsterdam, n.d.). The anti-discrimination policy was approved by the city council and is executed across all the responsible departments who co-ordinate with each other through regular meetings.

Multi-level governance of the reception and integration mechanisms for asylum seekers and refugees

Asylum seekers and refugee regulation

In the Netherlands, an agency of the Ministry of Justice called the Immigration and Naturalisation Service (Immigratie en Naturalisatiedienst, IND) assesses asylum applications and grants international protection status (i.e. subsidiary protection or refugee status) to humanitarian migrants on the basis of the Aliens Act (*Vreemdelingenwet*). In 2015, around 70% of all applications were approved (Gemeente Amsterdam, 2016b), compared with 51% in the EU28.

Several policy changes were made at the national level in 2014 with regards to asylum legislation. This was often directly related to the implementation of the Common European Asylum System and aimed at introducing more efficient admission procedures, including accelerated processing, earlier submission of claims at the initial registration process, and more favourable conditions for the family reunification of those who were granted refugee status. New guidelines were also implemented to improve the position of lesbian, gay, bisexual and transgender (LGBT) people in the asylum procedure (OECD, 2017a).

In general, the central government is responsible for the initial reception and related procedures, while local authorities focus on the long-term integration of refugees: competences over housing, education and health have been officially allocated to municipalities through the Increased Asylum Influx Administrative Agreement (2015) and supplementary agreements in 2016.

The Central Agency for the Reception of Asylum Seekers (*Centraal Orgaan Asielopvang)* COA[6] is responsible for asylum seekers while they are waiting for recognition of their status. However, in late 2015, the government devolved the responsibility for the provision of emergency shelters to the local authorities in the Netherlands in order to cope with the large influx of asylum seekers. Generally, asylum seekers stay in these emergency shelters for 6-12 months while waiting for a place in a regular asylum seeker centre (*Asielzoekerscentrum*, AZC). In 2014 and 2015, the COA increased the capacity of existing reception centres and opened 20 new (emergency/temporary) ones with a total capacity of nearly 10 000 beds (OECD, 2016h).

The COA distributes asylum seekers across the AZCs based on availability. Currently, asylum seekers are accommodated in the AZCs located throughout 90 locations in the Netherlands. Forthcoming OECD analysis on the presence of asylum seekers at the municipal level across OECD countries confirms that in the Netherlands asylum seekers are concentrated in towns and suburbs rather than in rural areas (OECD, forthcoming). The COA is in charge of managing the AZCs and decides where they will be established, but cities can apply for a centre, like Amsterdam did.

Amsterdam opened an AZC in August 2016 located in a former prison in the eastern part of the city that provides shelter for 1 000 people. Furthermore, two new centres were planned to open in the western part of the city in 2017 and 2019 to shelter about 500 people each. However, due to a lower[7] demand for shelter, one of these centres will most likely function as a bridging solution.

The centres provide asylum seekers with essential necessities such as food, clothing and medical care, defined by the "Regulation Care Asylum Seekers". There is no available estimation of the cost of hosting an asylum seeker in these centres. However, depending on the phase in the asylum-seeking procedure, an asylum seeker receives around EUR 58 per week for food and clothes. In certain cases, expenses are paid for kitchen utilities, public transport, education and particular healthcare needs. These measures are paid for by the central government. Sometimes it is also possible to earn some extra income by performing small jobs. However, asylum seekers are supposed to receive a deduction of their allocation in proportion to their income, up to 60% of the allocation.

Once a person is given a permit of stay based on international protection law, he/she is assigned to a municipality and leaves the AZC. The COA is again responsible for redistributing refugees across municipalities. If the Immigration and Naturalisation Service needs more time to decide on the request for asylum, asylum seekers begin the extended asylum procedure and stay at the asylum seekers' centre until the procedure is completed. If the asylum seeker has been refused a residence permit he/she may stay at the asylum seekers' centre for maximum four weeks. They can use this time to prepare for their departure from the Netherlands (Source: COA).

Criteria for dispersal are largely based on population size, that comes down to about 12 refugees per 10 000 inhabitants in 2016 (Geemente Amsterdam, 2016b). Every six months the central government decides how many permit holders each municipality must house. The COA selects a municipality based on a negotiation with the Association of Cities, and tries to match the skills/work experience of recognised refugees with labour market needs across the regions. To do this the COA has piloted a screening process (addressing issues such as: years of schooling, type of education, practised profession, etc.) that should be implemented across the country in 2017. Although the municipality is not officially involved in this process, there is a consultation for the actual allocation to dwellings in the city involving the COA, housing corporations and refugee mentors. The city of Amsterdam tries to influence the COA's decision by advocating that recognised status holders who spent time in the local AZC stay in the city.

Once recognised as a status holder, but still waiting at the AZC to be housed by the municipality, refugees receive a basic integration package funded by the COA, which includes 121 hours of Dutch classes and cultural background lessons, as well as coaching sessions. The respective municipality may also offer early integration opportunities such as studying, work or volunteer opportunities (for the case of Amsterdam see "The Amsterdam Approach Status-holders: Time applied to refugee integration" in Chapter 4).

Municipalities are required by law to provide housing (Housing Allocation Act [*Huisvestinsgwet*]) for those refugees allocated to them (see "Secure access to adequate housing (Objective 10)" in Chapter 6), and are also responsible for refugees' trajectory to settle in their city, including early measures related to the integration process in the sectors of education and access to the labour market. In Amsterdam the process of identifying and contracting a dwelling should take 2.5 days from the moment the refugee is assigned to the city. This delay has increased due to the increased demand in 2014.

Table 3.1. Which level of government exerts a role in refugee integration policies and to which extent is this role exercised in an autonomous way?

Function	City level	Intermediary level (province, state…)	Regional level	National level	Supranational or international level –including the EU
Policy setting	B			A	
Budget	B			A	D
Staff and other delivery processes	A				
Output (migrant integration policy delivery standards)	A				
Monitoring and evaluation of migrant integration policies	A			B	

Note: A: dominant role; B: important role; C: medium role; D: small role; E: blank/no role.
Source: Responses to the OECD questionnaire by the city of Amsterdam, 2017.

Table 3.2. Are the following policies competences of local governments?
Please tick the correct box for each

Policies	Local competency	Shared with other levels of government	Not a local competency
Number of refugees hosted by the city			X
Status of refugees hosted by the city			X
Housing for refugees	X		
Education for refugees	X		
Work authorisations for refugees			X
Health services for refugees	X		

Source: Responses to the OECD questionnaire by the city of Amsterdam, 2017.

Division of labour across city departments for reception and integration of status holders

Since 2015 the governance of the reception and integration of recognised status holders assigned to the city of Amsterdam is structured around the *"Amsterdam Approach Statusholders"* designed and implemented by the Unit of Work, Participation and Income (PWI) within the Social Services Department of the municipality. The concept and services delivered through the Amsterdam Approach Status holders will be explained in detail in "The Amsterdam Approach Status-holders: Time applied to refugee integration" in Chapter 4; this section focuses on the governance mechanisms for managing this approach.

The *Amsterdam Approach Statusholders* was officially approved by the City council in the course of 2016, identifying the areas of concern, policy priorities, and tangible measures regarding refugee integration. This approach pays special attention to vulnerable migrant groups such as children, unaccompanied minors, and people who are lesbian, gay, bisexual, transgender, queer or inter-sex (LGBTQI).

Since the increase of refugee inflows, a political decision was made to assign the response to the Work, Participation and Income PWI, which established partnerships within and beyond Amsterdam city services. Traditionally this unit had refugee integration amongst its competences but this represented only a small part of their business. In the wake of the inflows it was given a supplementary budget and mandate to set up a new approach. All relevant city services work together in a *chain* that has been defined as the *Programme Organisation Amsterdam Approach Status-holders* Initially a taskforce was established to coordinate all necessary activities across city departments, whereby every department took responsibility within the scope of their core business. Currently, the *Amsterdam Approach Status-holders* is predominantly executed and coordinated by *a team of civil servants from the key departments* (i.e., Work, Participation and Income and Economics), while the departments of Housing, Health and Education also have dedicated staff to support (see Figure 3.2). Lately the municipality has decided to set up a Refugee Department. The *Amsterdam Approach Status-holders* is largely implemented directly by the municipality, department WPI (70 case managers have been directly hired for this purpose; see "Build capacity and diversity in civil service, with a view to ensure access to mainstream services for migrants and newcomers (Objective 6)" in Chapter 5) in collaboration with different national and subnational partners: the COA, the Community Health Service (*Gemeentelijke Gezondheidsdienst*, GGD), housing associations, social welfare services, employers, as well as civil society initiatives who have a key role (Gemeente Amsterdam, 2015[7]). All these entities hold regular meetings with the aim of sharing information rather than join decision making.

After being assisted through tailored programme to integrate a work or education path during three years, if still in need, status holders are introduced to universal services offered by the municipality for youth or care programs specialised on multiple problems. There is a close collaboration between these universal services and the municipal teams in charge of the *Amsterdam Approach Status-holders* to ensure the beneficiaries are referred and receive follow up from the right general services.

Funding and costs

Funding was secured for 2016-17. The total budget for the Amsterdam Approach Status-holders (EUR 31.2-35.3 million) is covered by a municipal fund for innovative pathways to work and participation (EUR 10 million), with additional national funding following the increased influx of asylum seekers (EUR 17.2-21.3 million), and European co-financing from the ESF (EUR 4 million) that is managed by the Ministry of Social Affairs and Employment. The ESF and Asylum, Migration and Integration Fund (AMIF) funds covered 10-15% of the total cost of Amsterdam's integration measures. Specifically, Amsterdam recently applied for the AMIF, and for Employment and Social Innovation (EaSI) funding.

Ensure access to, and effective use of, financial resources that are adapted to local responsibilities for migrant integration (Objective 3)

In the Netherlands subnational governments' investment represents 50% of public investment (OECD, 2014a). The Netherlands scores well below the OECD average in terms of the share of subnational government tax revenues of total public tax revenue (OECD/UCLG, 2016).

For 2017, the city of Amsterdam has an estimated budget of EUR 5.7 billion. Subnational governments (especially municipalities) have a substantial budget composed of several streams. The volume of the funding stream from the central government to a municipality depends on the number of inhabitants with social needs, the number of houses, whether or not the municipality is a regional service hub, and its physical size. In 2017, Amsterdam received EUR 1.9 billion as a general grant. In principle, the central government has the power to intervene in the governance and functioning of subnational governments through the system of subnational government financing but in practice it seldom does (OECD, 2014). The city can allocate national grants as it wishes, with the exception of additional earmarked funding (EUR 660 million were provided to Amsterdam in 2017 for earmarked funding) that is meant for specific policy fields such as primary education or urban regeneration. About 45% of the city of Amsterdam's budget comes from central government funding. In addition, EUR 650 million is withdrawn from financial reserves, and about EUR 1.4 billion is generated from other sources in 2017.

In addition, municipalities have several own-source revenues, such as local taxes and administrative fees and charges (in Amsterdam this represented EUR 1.06 billion in 2017, or on average 16% of municipal income). The remaining funds stem from various other sources, such as European subsidies and municipal property (VNG, 2014). European funds are generally managed through the Ministry of Social Affairs and Employment (the provincial level is not involved).

As a result of the Participation Law (*Participatiewet*) adopted in 2015, municipalities now receive bundled funding (BUIG) for multiple social welfare regulations. Municipalities have discretion in the execution of these arrangements. Surpluses can be allocated elsewhere, while shortages have to be supplemented by the municipality itself. This mechanism provided an incentive for Amsterdam to help people become self-reliant as soon as possible, exceeding the target of lifting 4 200 persons out of the social benefit scheme and managing to help 6 000 persons in 2015.

Also in 2015, three laws changed[8] related to care, youth and work, leaving the municipality with more responsibility and approximately 25% less money than before when the state owned the process. This process was called 3d (3 decentralisation). Municipalities are in charge of the execution of these laws and have to find creative solutions to maintain more or less the same level of service, which includes key social services addressing migrants as well as other vulnerable groups. Yet, municipal officers estimate that the level of many services, especially those for the elderly and younger people, has decreased.

On the spending side, the City Council can spend local taxes as it wishes and has relative autonomy on the allocation of central funds. In 2017, most funding will go to mobility and urban space (EUR 1.2 billion); employment, income and community participation (EUR 1 billion); and city development and housing (EUR 0.8 billion). Furthermore, approximately EUR 544 million will be spent on education, youth and diversity. Moreover, in both 2017 and 2018 an additional EUR 2 million per year (0.03% of the total city budget) will be allocated specifically to refugee integration support (Gemeente Amsterdam, 2016a).

Key observations: Block 1

- Historically Amsterdam considered integration to be one of the city's top priorities. The 2013 Law on Participation reallocated some of the city's competences to the national level. The city reacted by increasing the provision of services to those migrants not targeted by the national package.
- Flexible national-local co-ordination mechanisms such as roundtables and financial incentives allow the higher level of government to advise and co-ordinate with the local level while still granting a great degree of local independence. A good example is the autonomy in designing refugee reception mechanisms as well as welfare and labour integration measures.
- The Association of Netherlands Municipalities (VNG) represents a unique structure for channelling municipal interests to the national level and ensuring two-way information flows. This has proven essential in managing the inflow of refugees effectively.
- There is no overall integration strategy as such: the city's approach is to privilege generic policies and promote equal access for migrants and refugees to public services and participation however adopting specific responses to groups when needs require. There is no integration unit in the municipality; co-ordination is ensured through informal interactions and a clear division of roles between departments in charge of related policies

Notes

1. Composed of 338 Dutch municipalities, the association supports the decentralisation process and facilitates decentralised co-operation.

2. The current test has four language skills components (speaking, listening, reading and writing), one component about Dutch society, and one about the Dutch labour market (the latter introduced in 2015).

3. If the test is passed the loan does not have to be reimbursed.

4. EU nationals, people who already passed their integration test and people above the age of 65.

5. www.miramedia.nl/media/file/Local-Welcome/Welcome-Europe-Toolkit_web.pdf.

6. As an administrative body, the COA falls under the political responsibility of the Ministry of Security and Justice.

7. Only 17 000 out of the 50 000 expected refugees after the EU-Tukey agreement in 2016.

8. The effect of the Participation Act superseded several social laws in January 2015. For instance, in the care sector the general law on exceptional medical expenses (Algemene Wet Bijzondere Ziektekosten) became the Social Support Act (Wet maatschappelijke ondersteuning), a new law was established for youth care and in the labour sector. Also the Work and Social Assistance Act (Wet Werk en Bijstand) benefits became part of the Participation Law (Source: www.cbs.nl/en-gb/about-us/contact/infoservice).

Chapter 4. Block 2. Time and space: Keys for migrants and host communities to live together

This section describes the leading principles of the city's reception and integration policies. Across the ten cities analysed in the case studies, the concepts of time and space appear to be essential in conceptualising sustainable solutions. Time is understood as the continuum in which solutions are executed in the city: from short-term reception and orientation, to long-term settling in the city along the key milestones of a migrant and his/her family lives. Space is understood as proximity and is well-illustrated by the word "connecting" (*Verbinding*) that the city has adopted in its approach to integration since 2003. Different communities can connect around spaces, activities, causes or housing solutions that facilitate regular interaction and break down prejudices and cultural barriers.

As it was expressed by city officers during the interviews with the OECD: *By itself, social cohesion is nothing, the main issue is where to find the connections between different communities; one can, for instance, look for these connections in a square, in a neighbourhood or at school. Finding these connections works indirectly against polarisation. It is important to find the right connections.*

It is becoming more and more evident that acquiring a host country's language and social norms as early as possible is essential to increase a migrant's or refugee's chances to find employment (Bakker, Davegos and Engbersen, 2013; OECD, 2017a). However, these skills are essential not only to newcomers, but also to other groups who might have been in the city for longer but failed to acquire them. In fact, access to almost every public service as well as participation depends on newcomers' language and cultural awareness. The city therefore considers it its role to fill the possible gaps left by national policies, in ensuring accessibility to universal services, economic and civic inclusion of migrants throughout their lifetimes. In doing so it operates within the margin available in the given legislative and financial framework; for instance, by ensuring that all groups of migrants have access to language classes throughout their lifetime (including EU migrants and migrants above the age of 65, including those who have already passed the test). Equally, the municipality supports "migrant-friendly" universal service provision: improving mediation and language skills of service providers. Sometimes it relies on the work of associations who provide targeted support for specific nationalities who then refer clients to relevant public services facilitating access to universal services (i.e. the municipality supports GGZ Keizersgracht, a Polish association providing Polish migrants with psychological care and supporting their referrals).

The integration process is conceived as mutual adaptation; therefore the city finds opportunities to create proximity between migrants and natives, who are both responsible for successful integration. For this purpose and for building support of the population for taking in and integrating with newcomers, communication with the citizens is one of the city's priorities (see Objective 2). Participation remains a key concept, along with participatory citizenship; for this purpose specific consultative mechanisms are in place (see Objective 5).

Design integration policies that take time into account throughout migrants' lifetimes and evolution of residency status (Objective 4)

The Amsterdam Approach Status-holders: Time applied to refugee integration

Box 4.1. The Amsterdam approach status-holders

The Amsterdam Approach contains a customised, holistic integration trajectory designed for each status holder. At the heart of the programme are case managers (the municipality appointed 70 case managers) who work together with job hunters and income consultants and colleagues from the Dutch Council for Refugees [Vluchtelingenwerk]. They coach status holders from the moment they receive recognition during the first three years in Amsterdam and develop an action plan for integration based on the refugees' qualities and talents, motivation, level of language acquisition, work experience, education, and overall mental and physical condition. Generally the action plan includes short-term and long-term objectives and includes finding work or education within the first six months. During this time, learning the language, receiving schooling and searching for work occurs simultaneously rather than sequentially. Such services are implemented by a plethora of non-state actors: University Assistance Fund (UAF) (see "Establish education responses to address segregation and provide equitable paths to professional growth (Objective 12)" in Chapter 6), Dutch Council for Refugees, Implacement, the NOA, etc. If external support is needed, case managers can refer refugees to further public services such as the Team Activation (Team Activering) or the Youthpoint centre (Jongerenpunt). Further referral options are neighbourhood activities based at community centres, such as the ones mentioned in "Strengthen co-operation with non-state stakeholders, including through transparent and effective contracts (Objective 7)" in Chapter 5. The implementation of the Amsterdam Approach is monitored by the municipal units in charge (Work, Income and Participation) as well as by control units and the case managers. The performance of all external partners involved in the implementation and the delivery of the outputs is formally tracked through a monthly dashboard. The framework includes concrete targets, i.e. 75% of refugee students under the contract between the municipality and the University Assistance Fund (UAF) (see "Establish education responses to address segregation and provide equitable paths to professional growth (Objective 12)" in Chapter 6) should complete their diploma within this programme

Language learning is a key component of the Amsterdam Approach. The intensive language course (Taalboost) is set up to advance access to work or education by teaching the essential linguistic skills relevant to the sectors of interest for the student. These trainings are tailor-made and groups are composed of a maximum four people (Gemeente Amsterdam, 2017). Furthermore, to facilitate civic integration, status holders are invited to an orientation programme, explaining Dutch norms and values, Dutch politics and the Dutch way of live. Other aspects include information about healthcare (e.g. hospital visits, personal

> hygiene, insurance) as well as orientation services, such as a visit to the public library and more about the history of Amsterdam. The orientation and language boost programme is provided by a non-governmental organisation called Implacement (www.implacement.nl).

The concept of time is clearly acknowledged in the Amsterdam Approach Status-holders. Based on past statistics, the approach acknowledged that refugees take considerable time to integrate and that many of them – on average 65% – were dependent on social welfare over the long term (Kennisplatform Integratie and Sammenleving, 2016).

The Amsterdam Approach Status-holders represents the city's attempts to do things differently. The concept of time was found to structure the approach and integrate previous lessons learnt, that showed that a sequential strategy of first learning the language, then receiving an education and finally finding employment often results in late integration to the labour market – only 25% of migrants had a job 3.5 years after recognition (Amsterdam Municipality). All of the measures introduced aimed at stimulating refugees' activity from a very early stage, taking a holistic point of view whereby different aspects of the integration process are actively stimulated from the beginning (including through early guidance towards employment or education, and civic and language courses). Still, social workers and city officers are aware that a refugee might experience a backlash once the three years come to an end and he/she is confronted with the difficulties of finding sustainable employment. The municipality has already successfully advocated for accompanying refugees during three years from their recognition and could consider some sort of sunset clause to accompany them as they evolve into self-sustenance and the universal care system.

Create spaces where the interaction brings migrant and native-born communities closer (Objectives 5)

Space applied to refugee integration

The Amsterdam administration includes the notion of space and proximity when designing innovative ways of involving the local and long standing migrant communities in activating refugees. The aim is to develop a network that links refugees with their new community. In the words of one of the refugees interviewed, "we want to be able to swim alone and feel a sense of ownership of the new environment where we are settling".

Proximity to and involvement of the local civil society are key factors for integration. There is a myriad of local, bottom-up initiatives in Amsterdam that help newcomers finding their ways into the city as well as establishing spaces that offer meeting points for migrants, refugees and natives. The municipality supports most of these initiatives either through funding or by providing free spaces.

Box 4.2. Providing space for integration: Examples of bottom-up initiatives

Meevaart is a communal centre located in one of the neighbourhoods with the highest concentration of migrants and refugees. The neighbourhood association created Meevaart Ontwikkelgroep (MOG), a foundation focusing on providing activities by and for neighbourhood residents. It contains a café and 12 classrooms that offer hospitality to migrants, locals and refugees to meet, drink, eat, chat, play and organise all sorts of activities and training. Activities that promote the social integration of different target groups are given priority. Many organisations, subsidised by the municipality, can rent the Meevaart classrooms to conduct their activities and this is how the centre covers its costs. The Meevaart space forms an important part of the community in the area, sustaining social cohesion and advancing the integration of different generations of migrants and refugees with the native community.

In collaboration with the city of Amsterdam, the Agency for the Reception of Asylum Seekers (COA) opened an asylum centre (AZC) in August 2016. This AZC is located in the eastern part of the city and was formerly a prison. It provides shelter for 1 000 people and in March 2017 hosted about 600. Inside the AZC, 72 entrepreneurs/incubators have been offered working spaces with the intention to provide opportunities for refugees to connect with the local business community. This creative hotbed, called Lola Lik, is freely accessible and offers room for events organised by volunteers in the realm of refugee integration (www.lolalik.nl).

The Refugee Talent Hub also has an office in the building. This is a platform sponsored by the municipality and private companies such as Accenture and IKEA, aiming to bridge the gap between employers and refugees. The Refugee Talent Hub screens refugees who have to prepare a digital portfolio based on their professional past and personal characteristics. The hub then matches these talents to potential employers based on a specifically designed algorithm. Launched early in 2017, by February of the same year there were 500 profiles online and 15 people had been placed. The Refugee Talent Hub has about 70 professional partners, of which most are small and medium-sized enterprises. The national government is also involved, providing support via its professional network. The hub further encourages the development of skills and competencies through "meaningful waiting activities", like language training and internships.

Another example is Boost Ringdijk. Established in 2015, Boost Ringdijk is a temporary work and meeting space for refugees and local residents. Through different activities (language and conversation classes, sports, shared workspaces, informative workshops about finding your way in Dutch society, music, dialogue and lectures, cooking and eating), groups meet and can learn from each other. Boost Ringdijk is located in the eastern part of Amsterdam and organised by both refugees and natives. Boost Ringdijk has proven to be a very successful formula. Its language teams have grown bigger and bigger. It currently has about 20 teachers, all volunteers. From the beginning, about 400 students have been enrolled. A lot of them take these classes in addition to the paid courses that third-country nationals have taken to pass the civic integration exam, through loans from the national government. There is also a language café where local people can have conversations in Dutch with newcomers on any topic. Furthermore, people can join drama classes, where small dialogues are practiced. Refugee and immigrant chefs cook a free meal every day. There is also a women's group, as well as a barbershop. Boost Ringdijk is supported by the city of Amsterdam, which has provided a start-up fund of EUR 50 000 and free use of the building (except for energy and water bills). Boost Ringdijk also closely co-operates with the Dutch Council for Refugees, who refers refugees living in the area to the centre. Boost Ringdijk also receives a lot of support from private citizens and foundations, either in the form of funding or in kind (e.g. chairs, tables, bedding, food).

Finally, in 2015, a group of local volunteers (some of whom are tied to the Meevaart and Boost Ringdijk) initiated a special bottom-up project regarding the early integration of refugees in the eastern part of Amsterdam. Over a period of six months they hosted 30 refugees who were waiting for their houses in a vacant building. City alderpersons interceded with the COA to authorise the transfer of the refugees from the AZC to this special centre and the municipality ensured that it would find more permanent accommodation in the neighbouring area. The city of Amsterdam also found the location, which was an old public office building. Most of the costs for the transformation of the building and further living costs were covered by crowd funding via Facebook. One person was hired to assist the group with their daily needs and to monitor the general course of events in the house. From the very first day, the children were able to join the local public school. After about seven months, almost all of the residents had been allocated housing in the direct neighbourhood. Despite the success, it is not likely that this project will be repeated. It was very costly and labour intensive and in general the provisions in shelters have improved. Furthermore, the need for refugee shelter is not as urgent as it was in 2015.

Consultative mechanisms to ensure migrants and refugees participation

Beside a regular survey to assess the opinion of non-western migrants living in the city (described in "Intensify the assessment of integration results for migrants and host communities and their use for evidence-based policies (Objective 8)" in Chapter 5), Amsterdam has established two bodies for consultation on integration issues. An independent Advisory Board on Diversity and Integration, composed of experts, and the Diversity Council (Stedelijk Overleg Diversiteit, SOD). Prior to 2004, an advisory board was made up of representatives of immigrant associations from a number of immigrant groups – Turks, Moroccans, Surinamese/Antilleans, Chinese and Pakistanis. Now the Diversity Council works as a public enquiry organ: based on interviews with municipal departments, relevant (migrant) organisations and involved residents, it prepares advice. This organ meets with the Advisory Board on Diversity and Integration about four times a year. The Board makes use of external experts and desk research. Once the advice is officially determined, it is offered to the College of Mayor and Alderpersons, who generally act upon it. It is further distributed to the City Council, relevant organisations and individuals, and the press (www.amsterdam.nl). In February 2017 the city established the Amsterdam Refugee Advisory Board. This body advises the municipality on the activities and communication oriented towards refugee groups.

Similar consultation mechanisms also exist in the city districts: for instance, the city district Oost-Watergraafsmeer has a board of representatives of migrant associations (BOMO) that meets five to six times a year, and establishes work groups on issues that are important for immigrants (Van Heelsum and Penninx, 1999). An issue oriented consultative mechanism is the so-called "soundboard group" (*klankbordgroep*), which can be alternatively described as a focus group for health professionals. This sound-board group is set up at the municipal level, and the main objective is to let key persons from different ethnic communities give their advice to professional care takers (see details in Objective 11).

Key observations: Block 2

- The Amsterdam Approach: the city adopted a holistic view whereby different aspects of the refugee integration process are actively stimulated from the beginning. This represents a deviation from the "mainstreaming universal access approach" to integration that the city implemented with other vulnerable groups.
- If this approach proves effective for rapidly steering newcomers into professional and education paths, it could be extended to other vulnerable groups, including second- and first-generation migrants.
- The city has been able to bring the local community on board for receiving and integrating refugees. Amsterdam structured bottom-up initiatives oriented at favouring exchange between different communities. This appears to be more developed than in the majority of other cities.
- The city is experimenting with innovative ways to include migrants and refugees in decision making which could be replicated elsewhere.
- Direct communication with citizens on practical reception and integration issues was effective in managing acceptance problems.

Chapter 5. Block 3. Local capacity for policy formulation and implementation

Build capacity and diversity in civil service, with a view to ensure access to mainstream services for migrants and newcomers (Objective 6)

Increasing diverse ethnic composition of the staff of all municipal institutions and companies at all levels serves two objectives: to reflect the characteristics of the city's population and to improve services' accessibility for migrants. Since beginning of the 1980s, the Amsterdam administration formulated a personnel policy providing that 17% of the municipal staff should have a non-western migrant background. Since 1991, the Regulation of the Legal Position of the Municipality of Amsterdam (Rechtspositieregeling van de Gemeente Amsterdam, RGA) includes an article on diversity policy, under the heading 'positive action' (CLIP, 2009[8]). In 2017 the city started a programme to hire refugees with the aim on one side to further increase the diversity of its personnel while on the other to give the example to local employers. A group of 14 refugees from Iran, Egypt, Syria and Eritrea started working for the municipality for a three-year programme, and after two years, will receive a contract. A combination of learning the Dutch language and gaining work experience is at the core of the programme.

Further capacity is built by exchanging practices around migrant integration with other cities. The city of Amsterdam has several formal and informal ties with international cities, meant to express solidarity and responsibility sharing, to exchange knowledge and/or to support each other in various domains. Across these international city networks Amsterdam is an active hub for sharing knowledge around migrant integration, and advises several partner cities who are experiencing similar challenges. For instance the city of Athens has a regular communication flow on several projects with the city of Amsterdam.

One example of the key role that Amsterdam undertakes in international knowledge management and advocacy around migrant and refugee integration is the **Urban Agenda for the European Union Partnership on Inclusion of Migrants and Refugees**. The city of Amsterdam and the Directorate General Migration and Home Affairs (DG HOME) of the European Commission are currently co-ordinating this initiative. The focus of the partnership is to improve access to European funding, improve EU-regulations and promote knowledge exchange. Two of the eight actions that the partnership developed have a focus on funding, is considering the scope to create financing facilities through which AMIF, ESF and potentially other EU funds could be blended with European Investment Bank (EIB) loans and thus made directly available to cities and financial intermediaries to implement investments in specified areas concerning migrant and refugee inclusion.

Other actions cover: housing, integration, and the provision of public services, social inclusion, education and labour market measures. Members are the cities of Athens,

Barcelona, Berlin and Helsinki; the national governments of Denmark, Greece, Italy and Portugal; as well as EUROCTIES; the Council of European Municipalities and Regions (CEMR); URBACT; the European Council on Refugees and Exiles (ECRE); the European Investment Bank; the Migration Policy Group; and two Directorates-General of the European Commission: Regional and Urban Policy (DG REGIO) and Employment, Social Affairs & Inclusion (DG EMPL).

Strengthen co-operation with non-state stakeholders, including through transparent and effective contracts (Objective 7)

The city recognises the added value in outsourcing services specifically targeting migrants and refugees to co-operatives, migrant associations or non-governmental organisations (NGOs) who have specific experience with these target groups. For instance, the city uses external partners to put in place programmes for the emancipation of women and vulnerable youth. Furthermore, many civil society organisations are supported by the municipality in their efforts to provide language courses to migrants and refugees (e.g. the Meevaart).

Such co-operation is usually established through grant agreements or an open procurement process. Generally, grant agreements imply more autonomy for the partner organisation. The procurement department within the municipality handles procurement contracts and monitors their execution together with the relevant policy staff. Challenges for funding involve lengthy bureaucratic application procedures and the need to formulate proposals that require a certain experience and resources are often only available for established associations.

Box 5.1. Examples: Founding sources for integration

In the past Amsterdam used two important sources of subsidies: the **Integration and Participation Subsidy** as well as the **Good Ideas Centre (MGI)**. Providing grants to associations between EUR 15 000 and EUR 50 000, the MGI procedure is considered a good example due to its fast process and direct link to the Mayor's office.

With regard to the implementation of the Amsterdam Approach, the external partners involved were selected through public procurement or a direct assignment for the delivery of a service.

In the past the municipality funded ethic- and religious-based organisations, including supporting structural costs such as rental or building maintenance. There has recently been a shift and the municipality no longer targets migrant associations but rather funds projects through call for proposals, related to integration and participation. Most of the regulations for applying for funding are directly linked to the municipal policy's goals of stimulating participation, social cohesion and integration.

Intensify the assessment of integration results for migrants and host communities and their use for evidence-based policies (Objective 8)

Monitoring integration outcomes

An annual report on integration in the Netherlands called the Jaarrapport integratie is published by Statistics Netherlands (CBS). The monitoring includes indicators on: demography, education, labour, income, benefits, crime, health and social participation. The 2016 report collected specific data on refugee groups. A number of specific themes are analysed more in-depth in the report: the results of migrants in more flexible segment of the labour market, the regional origin and settlement of Polish migrants who arrived since 2004, and the score on the Central Final Test of students with diverse backgrounds.[1]

The city produces a statistic report every two years "Amsterdam in cijfers"[2]- Amsterdam in numbers- which includes some information on the stock of migrant in the city. In 2004, 2007 and 2010 the city published the Diversity and Integration Monitor, to reflect the state of development of integration and diversity in the city of Amsterdam[3]. This has been expanded into the Scorecard Citizenship and diversity (see below) and for the first time a new version, the *Diversity Monitor,* has been published in 2017 as an interactive dashboard.[4] Produced by the Information, Research and Statistics Department of the municipality - *Onderzoek, Informatie en Statistiek (OIS)* these reports contribute to the city *Human Rights Agenda* (see "City vision and approach to integration" in Chapter 3) to ensure that all citizens of Amsterdam are able to fully participate in society. The Diversity monitor compiles different sources, including local survey data, local registration data and national registration data, to describe the situation of different groups in the city through 30 indicators regarding participation and conditions for participation. These indicators are grouped into three themes: equality of opportunity (health, social networks, societal inclusion); (conditions for) participation (socioeconomic position, societal/political participation); and living conditions. The dashboard allows to compare these indicators for groups of inhabitants disaggregated by: gender, age, level of education, immigrant background and residential neighborhood.

In addition since 2016 the city publishes every six months a specific monitoring on refugees the 'Vluchtelingenmonitor'[5] (Geemente Amsterdam, 2016b[9]). Several outcomes are monitored including: demographical and socioeconomic indicators, participation, health and welfare, housing, and public support. A combination of registration and survey data is used.

The municipality also commissioned in the past specific studies for instance on gaps in migrant education. One of the concerns raised by some of the city functionaries met during the OECD field visit is around the use of the information produced by the political level of the municipality. Although most of research is commissioned to the OIS by a policy department, it seems that mechanisms to ensure that policy makers use the results of the research to inform policies could be strengthened.

Perception surveys

Surveys have been conducted every three months since 2015 by the Information, Research and Statistics Department of the municipality to monitor the support for the reception and housing of refugees in the city. In general, the surveys reveal a positive perception of the way the municipality handles the reception and accommodation of asylum seekers and refugees. Only 6% of the respondents were unsatisfied.

The city published in 2013 a Score Card Citizenship and Diversity for 2009-2011.[6] This card includes indicators on how and to what extent residents perceive discrimination in the city. Data are be provided on the degree to which non-western residents, women and youth are economically independent, trust in democracy, and feel part of the city (Gemeente Amsterdam, 2016a).

Monitoring and evaluation of the Amsterdam Approach Status-holders

The city monitors how the Amsterdam Approach promotes integration of refugees in particular through the labour market, how these measures bring better results compared to the ones adopted in the past or to more bottom-up approaches, and if they could be replicated for other groups. As mentioned the implementation of the programme is closely measured through a monthly dashboard. In terms of impact evaluation, the municipality outsourced a research programme 'Vakkundig aan het werk' (skillfully at work) to Regioplan and the City of Amsterdam. 'Vakkundig aan het werk' is a joint programme of various government bodies and is aimed at providing municipalities (and practitioners) with evidence based knowledge on what works for whom and why in the field of labour market (re-)integration, poverty reduction and debt counselling. One of the target groups of this programme are refugees (i.e. beneficiaries of international protection).

The research grant allows for an in-depth study of the outline and content of the Amsterdam Approach Status-holders, the actual implementation of the programme and the effectiveness of the programme in terms of labour market insertion and enrolment in education. The study specifically focusses on the role of case-managers and job-hunters and on instruments such as the skills assessment, the intensive language training courses (Language boost) and the introductory programme (providing information on the city, the health care system and Dutch society).

To study the impact and results of the Amsterdam Approach Status-holders a realistic evaluation design is carried out[7]. In the first year the policy theory/intervention logic behind the Amsterdam approach was reconstructed and a process evaluation was carried out that will be public by January 2018. In 2018 a quantitative effect study will be carried out on the basis of register data with data on interventions and outcomes. This analyses will be followed by qualitative data collection among refugees and practitioners aimed at gaining insight into the explanatory factors behind the achieved results (what works for whom and why).

Finally, Amsterdam has contracted a specialised economics cabinet (LPBL) to produce a cost-benefit analysis every six months (see Box 5.2).

Box 5.2. Cost-benefit analysis of the Amsterdam Approach Status-holders

The municipality of Amsterdam uses cost-benefit analysis more often to evaluate and optimize policy, including policies for social care and welfare policies. The cost-benefit analysis takes in account all extra costs of the activities for refugees: client-management, extra activities (such as language boosts and internships) and programme management. It sets these against all the extra benefits, such as less unemployment-benefits, more taxes, more educational benefits (long term) and more quality of life. The results for the first year of the implementation (the new approach started as of July first 2016) were produced using a sample of

---

1 500 refugees (the so called 'Entrée-group'). The results of this group were compared with the results of a control-group (historical data) of over 3 000 refugees. The analysis shows that the employment rate after one year in the Entrée-group is 15% higher than in the control group (6%) and that employment comes earlier. The estimate of expected employment in the years to come is (according to the most ambitious of the three scenarios calculated) that 50% of the refugees doesn't need unemployment benefits within three years. Corrected for education, moving and other reasons for not needing unemployment benefits anymore, it means that within three years 25% of the refugees need to be employed. All costs and benefits considered the benefits exceed the costs by 50% in the basic scenario. It means that every euro invested leads to € 1.50 gained. In the potential scenario this is € 2.00 and in the ambition scenario € 3.00.

Source: Cabinet LPBL training en advies

Notes

1. www.cbs.nl/integratie.

2. www.ois.amsterdam.nl/pdf/2016%20jaarboek%20amsterdam%20in%20cijfers.pdf.

3. https://ec.europa.eu/migrant-integration/librarydoc/diversity-and-integration-in-amsterdam-monitor-2010.

4. www.ois.amsterdam.nl/visualisatie/dashboard_diversiteit.html.

5. www.ois.amsterdam.nl/nieuwsarchief/2017/vluchtelingenmonitor-voorjaar-2017.

6. www.ois.amsterdam.nl/nieuwsarchief/2013/scorekaart-burgerschap-en-diversiteit-2009-2011.

7. www.regioplan.nl/publicaties/slug/type/lopende%20projecten/slug/versnelde_participatie_en_integratie_van_vluchtelingen_de_amsterdamse_aanpak_deelrapport_i_werkwijze_en_beleidstheorie.

Chapter 6. Block 4. Sectoral policies related to integration

Match migrant skills with economic and job opportunities (Objective 9)

The Netherlands has the largest gap in labour market outcomes between native and foreign-born in the OECD. The gap in the unemployment ratio between native and foreign-born people was 14.4 percentage points in 2015, while the OECD average was 3.4 (OECD, 2017e). According to OECD database on migrant population outcomes at TL2 level, the gap in North Holland in the unemployment rate between native-born (6%) and foreign born (10%) was smaller in 2014-2015 than at national level. In 2016, the difference between the percentage of the unemployed population in Amsterdam among non-western migrants (10.2%) and native born (4.7%) was 5.5 percentage points (OECD, 2017e). An OECD Skills review (OECD, 2017e) for the Netherlands shows that even within the same level of education, the employment gap between the native and foreign-born populations persists, hinting at the fact that other factors such as discrimination, difficulties in the recognition and validation of skills, as well as social and economic networks might play a role in labour market performance.

According to the information provided by the city, several measures have been taken to increase migrant integration through labour. Monitoring the immigrant to native-born ratio of employees has been possible since the 1990s when the national government obliged employers to register all employees, including migrants. In those years, employers in Amsterdam set up a foundation which aimed at helping immigrants obtain a stable job.

While the city doesn't have the competence to decide on labour migration policies and working permits, which are under the remit of the national government, it plays a vital role in influencing job placement and can help to connect newcomers as well as long-standing resident migrants and local employers. The city indicates to be greatly involved in the qualification and education of migrants, which are a prerequisite for successful entry to the labour market. Further, the city plays a role in welfare benefit distribution as it distributes social benefits to 40 000 unemployed people through financing from the Ministry of Social Affairs and Employment. Among these beneficiaries approximately 77% have a migrant background (OECD-Questionnaire, Amsterdam, 2017). Migrants generally benefit from the services of the employment insurance agency (Uitvoeringsinstituut Werknemersverzekeringen) on the same basis as nationals, provided they have previously worked in the Netherlands. Specific measures that the city takes will be analysed below.

High-skilled labour

The demand for high- and medium-skilled workers substantially exceeds supply in the Dutch labour market: until 2025, 1.3 million new job opportunities are expected at medium skill levels and 2.4 million at high skill levels. During the same period, the labour supply is expected to grow by only 1 million for highly skilled people and to fall for medium skilled ones (OECD, 2016d). Based on these projections, a Highly Skilled Migrants Scheme, introduced in 2004 and revised in 2014, aims at attracting "knowledge" migrants. A facilitated procedure[1] allows Dutch companies to file visa applications for highly skilled migrants they would like to recruit from outside the EU (OECD, 2017a). Visa applications for "knowledge migrants" are accepted based on the remuneration they will receive, not on educational requirements. Therefore, it is possible that the first 7 000 permits for knowledge migrants issued in 2014 do not necessarily correspond to a higher share of tertiary educated persons among employed migrants nor that they have contributed to the highly innovative and export-oriented top nine sectors of the Dutch economy, where migrants are currently under-represented (OECD, 2017a).

The city of Amsterdam has deployed significant efforts to attract skilled migrants and has made contacts with local enterprises to this end. The city established the Expat Centre (now called IN Amsterdam – International Newcomers Amsterdam): a one-stop shop for the integration of highly skilled migrants. Migrants find assistance to register and settle in the city. In collaboration with the national Ministry of Security and Justice (Immigrate and Naturalisation service, IND) the Expat Centre helps with residence and work permits, registration with the municipality, tax questions and many other official matters.

Support to groups that face obstacles in entering or re-entering the labour market

In 2015, non-western migrants were three times more often unemployed than natives, and 1.5 times more so than EU migrants (OECD-Questionnaire, Amsterdam, 2017). This population is part of the group facing obstacles to entering or re-entering the labour market that the municipality targets through a set of measures.

The programme "Amsterdam Inclusive Labour" market has been developed by local authorities with the aim of creating professional networks that are willing to educate and employ migrants and refugees.

The ''Create your own job" (*Eigen Werk*) initiative is the city's programme to support unemployed people who would like to become entrepreneurs; 10-20% of its beneficiaries have a migration background. The programme has been running for over ten years and is part of a general re-integration policy – with a 70% success rate of starting a business. Success rates are similar between natives and migrants. "Create your own job" systematically maps in which sectors there are more opportunities for entrepreneurs to create a start-up. This mapping is done in collaboration with the Chamber of Commerce and the Statistics Netherlands, which provides data. As workshops in the programme are in Dutch, migrants should have a good command of the language. All programme participants are eligible for national tax benefits for entrepreneurs. Moreover, when applicable, authorities top up the entrepreneurial income to the amount of their initial unemployment benefit (based on their personal employment history) or social benefits (accessible to all) for up to three years. The city also provides microfinance for migrant entrepreneurs.

Refugees' integration in the labour market

Supporting refugees to find employment is a priority for the city under the previously described Amsterdam Approach. In the past the city observed that during the first three years after their arrival, less than 25% of refugees were employed. Yet, research shows that the chance of employment increases the longer a refugee resides in the Netherlands, thus encouraging policies to help refugees find a job in a shorter period of time

(Gemeente Amsterdam, 2016b). Specifically, low employment numbers are found for Somalis, Iraqi and Afghan refugees (Wittebrood, K. and I. Andriessen 2014). To target these issues, the Amsterdam Approach offers fast, intensive and high-quality language lessons combined with intensive coaching and guidance to enter different aspects of integration including health problems. The first step is to assess refugees' skills to orient them towards educational or professional opportunities. This was outsourced by the city to Manpower, a leading private headhunting company. Manpower implemented a pilot project in the AZC asylum centre in Amsterdam, which included the design of an assessment tool, in different languages, to identify the specific competences and aspirations of the candidates and defining a personal development plan. Most participants needed to focus on their level of Dutch in order to increase their chances in the labour market. Another pilot project is being implemented in the AZC camp to facilitate refugees' access to jobs – the Refugee Talent Hub[2] (see "Space applied to refugee integration" in Chapter 4). This is a digital matching platform sponsored by the municipality and private companies such as Accenture and IKEA, aiming to bridge the gap between employers and refugees. It is interesting to notice how companies, NGOs, educational institutes and the government who are involved in the platform proudly advertise their engagement through social media, contributing to establishing social recognition for welcoming refugees and helping them find a job.[3]

In October 2015, at the beginning of the influx of refugee and asylum seekers, the municipality developed an Action Plan in co-ordination with a number of stakeholders, among them: the Confederation of Netherlands' Industry and Employers (VNO-NCW), the COA, the IND, employment agencies, education/training institutions as well as universities. The action plan aimed at gaining insight on the competences of newcomers. It advocates for starting individual trajectories towards employment before status recognition and, concerning refugees, fostering a quick and suitable match between competences and employers (e.g. making use of acceleration programmes, partnerships and networking events).

It is important to note that the Amsterdam Approach represents an update of and creates synergies with previous initiatives for migrants developed in the city, including, for instance, the Access to Amsterdam programme *(Toegang tot Amsterdam)*. This project has existed since 2011 and comprises an integrated approach towards language, empowerment and employment skills. A first evaluation conducted in 2014 showed the programme pays off, with 73% of the participants moving one step up on the so-called participation ladder. Equally, the approach seeks synergies with the re-integration efforts of the Action Plan against Youth Unemployment (*Aanvalsplan Jeugdwerkloosheid*), the Action Plan for Entrepreneurship (*Actieplan Ondernemerschap*) and the programme Employment for and by Refugees (*Werk voor en door Vluchtelingen*), set up by the Ministry of Economic Affairs.

Secure access to adequate housing (Objective 10)

Social housing in the Netherlands is a competence mostly shared between the central government, the municipal level and housing associations. The central government sets the quality standards for new buildings, the regulatory framework for housing associations, the regulation for housing benefits and determines the number of status holders that each municipality should accommodate. The province has a very limited role in this sector and is mainly concerned with spatial planning for new housing. It also controls whether municipalities fulfil the housing quota for status holders. The municipality is in charge of housing for all vulnerable groups, including refugees. A unit in charge of housing is situated in the economic services department of the municipality, and co-ordinates the housing aspect of the refugee response (OECD-Questionnaire, Amsterdam, 2017).

Figure 6.1. Competences for social housing in Amsterdam

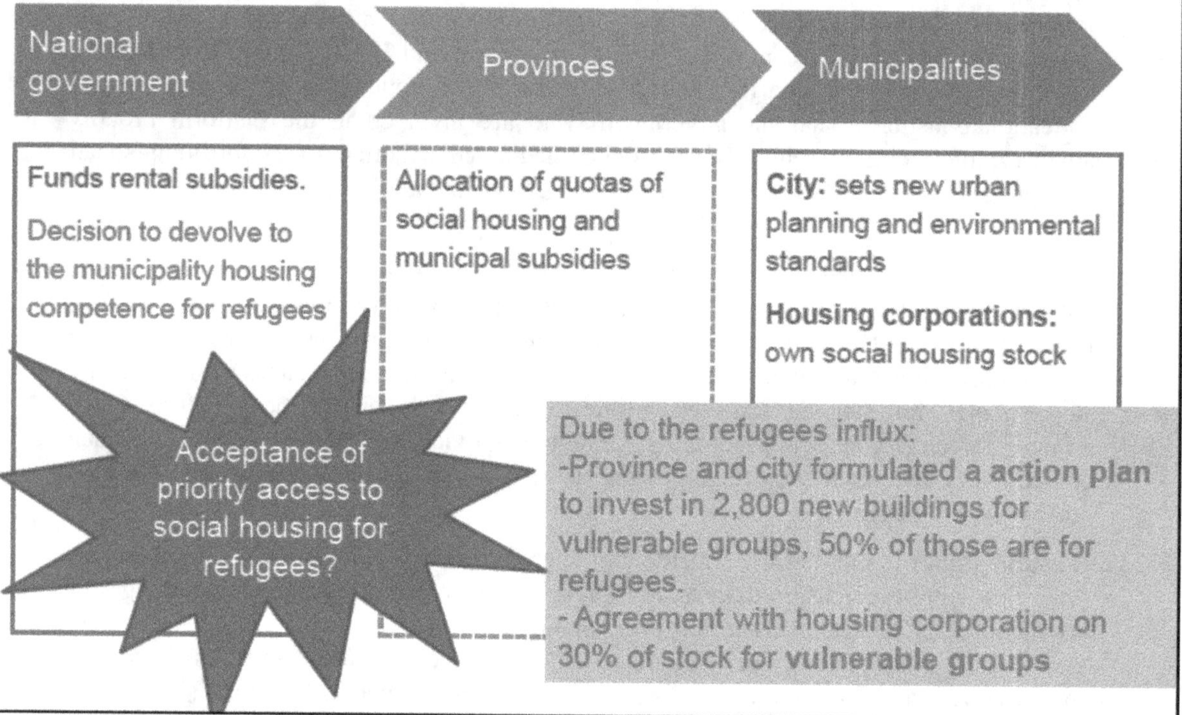

Source: Author's compilation based on responses to the OECD questionnaire Amsterdam, 2017.

The city of Amsterdam has an active land policy, meaning it is involved in releasing land for development and developing it itself (OECD, 2017g). The municipality also has its say in new housing projects in terms of urban planning. While direct funding for the construction of affordable housing is largely absent, municipalities can offer lower land prices to housing associations.

Amsterdam has six housing associations. These associations are non-profit organisations with their own board and they control their housing stock. They are responsible for managing social housing, investing in new buildings and dealing with social housing applications. They work based on a set of regulatory frameworks negotiated with the municipality and the tenants' associations on a range of issues such as: the environment, the distribution of housing, building and living standards as well as affordability. In the past housing associations were instrumental in building and renovating new neighbourhoods; the share of social housing stock reached 80% in the 1980s. Today housing associations' stock represents 43% of all housing in Amsterdam, 95% of which is in the social rental sector (OECD, 2017d).

Social houses (houses made available to dwellers paying a subsidised rent) are allocated to Amsterdam residents strictly on the basis of income: in 2016 households with an annual income lower than EUR 36 165 (before tax) were eligible. The maximum net monthly rent for social housing was EUR 710.68 in 2016, the average rental costs for social housing in Amsterdam in 2015 was EUR 496, compared to EUR 745 on average rent for private rentals (OECD 2017g). The income criterion applies to all residents equally. However, priority access is given to vulnerable groups including disabled citizens, victims of domestic violence and refugees. In 2015, the average registration time for accessing social housing was 8.7 years (Questionnaire Amsterdam, 2017).

Amsterdam has developed a housing strategy called "Vision 2020" to address the structural shortage of affordable housing. Amongst other targets the strategy aims at increasing the turnover in social housing stock (e.g. by increasing rents at a higher pace for tenants whose earnings have passed certain thresholds) and at building neighbourhoods where all groups – regardless of age, income and ethnicity – live together. The 2015 reform of the Housing Act introduced changes to the commercial activities of housing associations for instance by introducing a new levy but also making it easier for associations to sell portion of their housing stock to the private market. Generally, the city and associations express the idea of a "sustainable equilibrium" to balance the housing demand. At present this equilibrium amounts capped at 162 000 housing units own by associations. For further analysis of housing and real estate trends see *The Governance of Land-Use in the Netherlands: The Case of Amsterdam* (OECD, 2017g). Three factors seem to influence spatial distribution in the coming years, potentially making the inner city more and more polarised. On the one end is going to be increasingly inhabited by highly advantaged dwellers who can either buy the social housing stock now being privatised or who already own a property – 29% of dwellings in Amsterdam in 2015 were owner occupied (Geemente Amsterdam, 2016) – or who can afford high rents. On the other end, the inner city will be characterised by the most disadvantaged dwellers who benefit from the social housing system. In effect, since 2011 changes to national legislation have increasingly set higher rent for middle-income individuals, pushing them to move to the private rental market, often outside the inner city (OECD, 2017g). Finally, the city has competence for building neighbourhoods where all groups can co-exist and potentially the right to release the land for development.

Mechanisms for housing refugees in the city of Amsterdam

The inflow of refugees in 2014-15 created even more pressure on the city's housing system, as according to the Housing Allocation Act (*Huisvestinsgwet*, renewed in 2014), the municipality is responsible for providing accommodation for refugees allocated to its territory.

Recognised refugees assigned to the city of Amsterdam are placed in housing in collaboration with the COA, the housing associations and the refugee's case manager. In 2016, 2 013 refugees received social housing either through temporary rental contract or in an asylum centre. In addition, two measures were put in place: 1) an agreement was established between the municipality and the housing associations stating that 30% of available rentals should be allocated to vulnerable groups, including refugees, who represent roughly one-third of the beneficiaries; 2) the province of North Holland and the city of Amsterdam formulated an action plan to make up for the shortfall of housing for vulnerable groups, investing in 2 700 new dwellings until 2018. Funding mainly comes from the housing associations themselves and the municipality. National funding to build new houses for refugees is available, but the criteria are restrictive, i.e. four refugees should be hosted in one apartment. No European funds are being used at this time for this purpose.

The mechanism to assign long-term housing to recognised refugees is implemented by the municipal housing unit and the housing associations. All housing associations are involved in identifying available housing and make a "gentlemen agreement" for sharing equally the number of refugees who need to be sheltered, thus also allowing dispersion across different neighbourhoods, which avoids putting more pressure on neighbourhoods that already have an established presence of migrants and refugees. Once suitable housing becomes available, the housing associations and the municipality make a one-time offer (accept or decline) to the refugee. If the refugee accepts (which is almost always the case), he/she is provided with basic services and a grant to sum the house (partially a grant – EUR 600 – partially a loan – EUR 1 600). The municipality pays a loan to the housing association to cover the cost of the house. Refugees, as all other social housing dwellers, are supposed to pay the corresponding rent, but can receive financial support from the municipality if their income is insufficient. The national government funds these housing subsidies. The process of contracting the allocation, registering and moving from the AZC should take 2.5 days from the moment the refugee accepts the house. There is no time limit for refugees to stay in the dwelling. Tenants may officially swap dwellings, allowing them to move to other locations.

Refugees younger than 28 years old are eligible for student housing; however, these kinds of dwellings are only available for a maximum of five years. The housing associations match the student's skills and competencies to the residential environment in co-ordination with the municipal department in charge of education. Refugees housed as students are not accounted for in the 30% quota of social housing for vulnerable groups.

Provide social welfare measures that are aligned with migrant inclusion (Objective 11)

General social benefits

According to the data provided by the city of Amsterdam, in 2015, 13.8% of non-western migrants received social benefits, opposed to 2.2% of the native-born population and 4.4% among western migrants (Statistics Netherlands, 2016). The city also indicated that around 65% of recognised refugees – who represent 0.8% of the migrant population in Amsterdam – receive social benefits, compared to 7.7% of the Amsterdam population on average. Eleven to 15 years after arrival, dependency on social benefits among refugees is still five times higher than the average in Amsterdam. Some groups of refugees are more dependent on social benefits than others; for instance, after residing in the Netherlands for at least nine years, 23.9% of the Afghan migrants, 32.4% of the Iraqi migrants, 21.4% of the Iranian migrants and 43.2% of the Somali migrants received social benefits (Statistics Netherlands, 2016).

Box 6.1. Example of social support at the neighbourhood level

In terms of general social services, the municipality has implemented care programmes, like the "ACT together" (Samen DOEN) programme. This programme consists of 22 teams across the city specifically in charge of supporting inhabitants/families who are simultaneously facing several problems, such as with work, upbringing, debts, education, housing and healthcare. When needed, recognised refugees can be referred to these services. This programme depicts the integrated needs-based approach to public services that Amsterdam tries to offer to all users at the neighbourhood level.

Healthcare

Health statistics for Amsterdam indicate that natives are in better health than non-western migrants; in addition, healthcare costs are lower for natives and EU migrants than for non-western migrants. In particular, obesity and diabetes are a problem for non-western migrants (Statistics Netherlands, 2016). Depression and post-traumatic stress disorder can be a problem for refugees and asylum seekers; Statistics Netherlands estimates that between 13% and 25% of asylum seekers and refugees are treated for these diseases in the Netherlands. Yet, the general health of the recently arrived is good, as this group is mostly young and has shown resilience in dealing with the fleeing experience (Gemeente Amsterdam, 2016b). The health of some refugees even worsens during their stay in the Netherlands compared to their health when they arrived (Lamkaddem, Essink-Bot and Stronks, 2013). This is often related to the poor socio-economic situation of refugees, which lacks perspective and creates stress. It underlines further the need for early integration and health measures that the city could provide. Moreover, many migrants have insufficient knowledge about the Dutch healthcare system, which hinders their access to treatment.

This is why the municipality aspires to address these issues as early as possible. For example, more attention is now given to prevention by means of counselling on a healthy lifestyle (Gemeente Amsterdam, 2015).

To access basic health[4] in the Netherlands one needs to subscribe to a private health insurance company. Non-EU migrants have to subscribe after three months (once they receive a valid residence permit) and EU migrants after one year in the Netherlands. When the person is unemployed or does not have sufficient income to pay for the insurance, he/she receives a subsidy from the national government for as long as needed.

Some measures have been taken at the national level to respond to the influx of refugees. For instance, the Regulation for Asylum Seekers (*Regeling Zorg Asielzoekers*, RZA) gives asylum seekers in the asylum centres (AZC) access to healthcare that is highly comparable to the general basic healthcare insurance and long-term care insurance for Dutch residents and employees.

The COA is the body responsible for the provision of healthcare for asylum seekers. A few days after registration, asylum seekers receive an RZA healthcare card with a personal COA healthcare number. Once they are granted status they can subscribe to basic health insurance. In 2009, the COA externalised the provision of health services for RZA holders to a Dutch private health insurance corporation, Menzis. Services are provided at general practitioners centres (*Gezondheidscentrum Asielzoekers*, GC A) located near or at each AZC. Furthermore, asylum seekers have the right to an interpreter when seeking healthcare. This service has been commissioned to Concorde, a private translation company (www.concorde.nl), since 2015.

Public healthcare (*Publieke Gezondheidszorg Asielzoekers*, PGA) is provided by the Association of Community Health Services (GGD)[5] and Regional Medical Preparedness and Planning (GHOR) office. The GHOR is predominantly responsible for national co-ordination of the 25 Dutch GGD centres. The GGD centres usually operate in several municipalities, which give their own assignments to the GGD, as specified in the municipal memoranda on local policy on community health. These services are generic and the COA has an agreement to provide them specifically for asylum seekers. Since November 2016, the national government assists in the co-ordination of healthcare development and health programmes for refugees through the appointment of a regional health co-ordinator for each working area of the GGD. The regional co-ordination is funded by the national Ministry of Public Health, Welfare and Sports and will last at least until May 2018. *The goal is to achieve structural healthcare policies for migrants with a residence permit and to implement and embed this policy in the future strategies of the local authorities.*

Among others, the support from the regional co-ordination includes the sharing of national good practices, networking, the creation of a chain of care, and the provision of knowledge about healthcare that is culturally sensitive. In line with this, the VNG provides support and advice about policies that concern the health and well-being of migrants and refugees to local governments. Pharos, the Dutch Centre of Expertise on Health Disparities, provides counselling in this respect. In turn, the regional co-ordinator advises the municipality about the quality of care and cures. Currently, the city of Amsterdam is offered this overarching support together with five other smaller municipalities. The nomination of a regional health co-ordinator addresses several concerns that various organisations (e.g. NGOs, governmental organisations) had raised:

- achieve more effective policies through co-ordinated efforts
- underline the need for intercultural and professional education of healthcare professionals in order to enhance their competences in working with migrants and refugees
- more systematically address the prevention of health problems among refugees, including monitoring their health and socio-economic status more regularly and providing operators with longer contracts.

The regional health co-ordination on health provision for status holders and other migrants aims to systematically deliver more effective polices, share best practices, strengthen intercultural competences and prevent health problems. Municipalities are offered this overarching support on issues related to migrant health as well as from the VNG and the Dutch Centre for Expertise on Health Disparities.

Another example for co-ordination and sharing of best practices in health services dealing with refugees and migrants has been the implementation of a so-called "sounding board group" (*klankbordgroep*), which can be alternatively described as a focus group for professionals. This sounding board group is set up at the municipal level, and its main objective is to let key persons from different ethnic communities give their advice to professional care takers on how to approach the respective target group. Efforts are currently being made to integrate all relevant perspectives during the evaluation phase of a policy, while keeping the lines of communication between policy makers and practitioners as short as possible.

Establish education responses to address segregation and provide equitable paths to professional growth (Objective 12)

Historically the Dutch government's approach to migrants' education was to help them maintaining their own culture, in view of a possible return to their home country. Thus, from the 1970s the national government financed education systems for immigrant children in their own language and culture. Since the early 1980s, the Dutch Minister of Education changed the "minority language and culture teaching" policy objective from "encouraging re-migration" to "encouraging integration", recognising that temporariness was fiction. Since 1994, teaching took place in Dutch and language classes – of students' native language – were provided only outside of regular school hours. This programme stopped being financed in 2004 (Bouras, 2012).

Gaps in education attainment and results

As explained above, generally, non-western immigrants in Amsterdam have a lower overall educational attainment than native Dutch: for all levels of education, non-western migrants are less likely to obtain their degree than natives. Children from Turkish or Moroccan descent have significantly more difficulties passing language tests in primary schools. However, the percentage of non-western students that enrols in higher educational programmes has increased over the past decade, but this also holds true for native students. Thus, the overall educational attainment gap between non-western immigrants and natives remains nearly unchanged (Statistics Netherlands, 2016). Still, in terms of average score of students at the bottom of the performance distribution, students in the Netherlands have relatively high results compared to other OECD countries is. The OECD 2016 review of Dutch national polices for education showed that the performance gap between students with an immigrant background and native students is smaller in the Netherlands than in countries of a similar size and nature of migrant population (such as Austria, Germany or Sweden) (OECD, 2016d).

A number of reasons have been explored in the literature as contributing gaps in educational attainment and results.

The concentration of immigrant students in "enclave schools" has detrimental effects on learning; this is not due to the concentration of immigrant students, but because of the concentration of socio-economically disadvantaged students, for instance the educational levels of the children's parents (OECD, 2015). The parental choice system in the Netherlands is contributing to creating more segregated schools. (Ladd, Fiske and Rujis, 2009). Two important policy options to balance school choice are the strengthening of weak schools to ensure making quality education accessible for all and to enhance the means of disadvantaged and migrants families to exercise a well informed choice (OECD, 2010).

Means deployed by municipal authority to improve quality education for all groups

Municipalities operated public schools until 2006, when they were made the responsibility of independent boards, thus leaving local policy makers with no operational authority. All schools are subject to the same national accountability standards, general national curriculum guidelines and national teacher salary schedules (Ladd, Fiske and Rujis, 2009). Primary schools receive equal funding regardless of whether they are publicly (30% of Dutch primary students attend public schools) or privately operated

Municipalities tried to tackle the school selection mechanisms to influence the parental choice system. For instance, some municipalities in the Netherlands (i.e. Nijmegen) have introduced a central subscription system to assign students to primary schools, so as to reach a share of 30% of disadvantaged students in each school. In other cities (i.e. Rotterdam), oversubscribed schools are required to give preference to children who would enrich the school's ethnic and socio-economic mix (OECD, 2010b).

Efforts have been made to attract more funding for schools serving disadvantaged students, so as to improve the educational achievement of primary/grammar school pupils and thus access for these students to higher forms of secondary education. From 1973 to 2006, a national "weighted funding" system (*gewichtenregeling*) aligned the level of funding to the school for each child based on the educational attainment and ethnicity of his/her parents (Vink, 2008). The ethnicity clause was dropped in 2006 and now funding is only based on the parents' educational attainment.

Currently, a national policy is being implemented by municipalities which directly target the access of disadvantaged children (which includes immigrant children according to the target definition of this policy) to quality early education and care. Early childhood programmes (day care centres, pre-kindergardeten and kindergarten, up until the age of six) can offer what is referred to in the Netherlands as "before and early school education" (*voor en vroeg schoolse educatie*, VVE) for students with a migration background in addition to the general education programme. These programmes have been implemented since the early 2000s and funded by municipalities, with the objective to reduce the integration gap very early, by providing, in particular, language support (OECD, 2016d). One study proved that increased investment in VVE reduces repeating a year during the first two years of primary school (at age four or five), which is heavily biased towards children from socio-economically disadvantaged and immigrant backgrounds (Akgunduz and Heijnen, 2016). Nowadays, early childhood education is funded by the central government and distributed by the municipal authorities (preschool VVE) and school boards (VVE in primary education) (Eurydice, 2017).

The municipality is also involved in skills recognition and works with NUFFIC, a non-profit Dutch organisation in charge of the recognition of qualifying degrees in the Dutch system. NUFFIC matches the level of education previously obtained in the country of origin with the Dutch requirements and indicates the amount of additional courses needed to obtain an equivalent professional degree. Information about assessing foreign qualification is also systematically provided in the integration programme for immigrants that is offered within the framework of the civic integration exam (OECD, 2017b).

Refugees' integration through education

Strategies for education and training of newcomers in Amsterdam started well before the peak in arrivals of refugees and asylum seekers. In 2009, the city developed a strategy based on the results of a study it had commissioned on the educational needs and profiles of newcomers. This strategy was expanded as the number of newcomers increased in 2015, by increasing the number of partners involved in its implementation.

Since the increase of the number of refugee arrivals, 114 elementary and secondary schools have received new refugee students. The city organises newcomer classes for children 6-11 years old to ensure their level of Dutch is sufficient to join regular education. To that end, the city receives a budget for schooling refugee and asylum seeker students 5-18 years old. The money has been used to hire more teachers and build new classrooms. However, the duration of the funding is uncertain, leaving the programme largely open.

Within the framework of the Amsterdam Approach, refugees above the age of 18 who hold a master degree have the opportunity of completing or validating their higher education. The municipality has established a contract with the UAF[6] which supports refugees in their procedures with NUFFIC for the recognition of their diplomas and connects graduated refugees to the labour market as early as possible. Students under this scheme are provided with a scholarship and coaching. According to the target set by the Amsterdam Approach, 75% of the students under this programme should complete their diploma.

For refugees with an intermediate level of education, the main objective of the Amsterdam Approach is for them to acquire a basic qualification. In general, refugees older than 18 but under 28 are oriented towards an education path. For instance, the city organises bridging classes that allow refugees to start their bachelor's degree. The target is that 50% of those who receive training will complete this successfully. This is implemented in co-operation with regional education centres (*Regionale Opleidings Centra*, ROCs), that mostly offer intermediate vocational training, and Dutch as a second language courses. For lower or uneducated refugees, who receive a social allowance, the focus is on basic language training and citizen participation (a dual trajectory). This is a multi-year path that is customised towards specific educational needs and that also includes participatory programmes.

Key observations: Block 4

- The national-local co-ordination mechanism in the health sector is significant not only as example of multi-level-governance, but also as an example of how updates in service delivery and related governance mechanisms implemented to respond to refugee inflows can be extended to larger groups, including long-standing migrants. From only sharing knowledge, this mechanism could be scaled up to actual service provision. A good example could be the collaboration between 13 municipalities in the Gothenburg region that share responsibility for migrant service provision across the province.
- The "Amsterdam Inclusive Labour Market" programme and the Refugee Talent Hub are examples of the city's efforts in building networks with professionals that are willing to educate and employ migrants and refugees, and not only the high-skilled ones. These experiences need to be well documented in order to decide if is worth scaling them up,
- Efforts to accurately assess refugees' competences early on show that the city has learned from unsuccessful labour integration of large groups of refugees in the past. It could also systematise its efforts to match profiles with local opportunities – beyond the Refugee Talent Hub – by establishing regular dialogue with the chamber of commerce and the Institute for Employee Benefit Schemes (UWV). One example is the Austrian collaboration between the Employment Agency and the chamber

---

of commerce for matching refugee profiles with the right job opportunity also beyond Vienna.

- The city's response to housing refugees and asylum seekers is an example of successful multi-level co-ordination. It also shows the city's resilience capacity: the city recognised hosting refugees as a priority and collaborated with other stakeholders (housing associations, COA, etc.) to find appropriate housing solutions. It also shows its communication capacity by sensitively explaining its decision to the public. The response took into account spatial distribution, thus avoiding the concentration of newcomers in more disadvantaged neighbourhoods.

- Across-the-board services have been updated to respond to refugee arrivals since 2015. These targeted responses in the field of housing, labour, health and education, as well as the governance innovations that accompanied them (i.e. the chain model to implement the Amsterdam Approach) should be considered as pilots and through close monitoring the city could evaluate the feasibility of extending it beyond this group, which only represents 0.8% of the population with a migration background in the city.

- The municipality has limited competences in addressing the education gaps between students with migration background and the rest of the population. However some measures implemented through local authorities in early and pre-school education show promising results in reducing repetition of years in primary school. The tailored approach to the level of education of newcomers conceived within the Amsterdam approach as well as the decision to disperse them across 114 schools in the city are promising and their impact in terms of accelerating learning process should be monitored.

Notes

1. Employers need to become a "recognised sponsor" by registering with the Dutch Immigration Service and pay a fee of EUR 5 276 (lower for start-ups and companies employing less than 50 people). The approval is valid for an indefinite period and allows the company to file visa and work permit applications (https://ind.nl/en/work/pages/highly-skilled-migrant.aspx).

2. www.refugeetalenthub.com/en/werknemers/home/#/inspiratie.

3. www.matchcare.nl/proud-partner-refugee-talent-hub.

4. Two main forms of healthcare insurance exist in the Netherlands: basic insurance that covers common medical care (Zorgverzekeringswet, Zvw) and insurance against long-term nursing and care for people with chronic illnesses, vulnerable elderly, or people with a severe mental or physical handicap (Wet langdurige zorg, Wlz). Dutch residents and employees are automatically insured against long-term care by the government, but everyone is obliged to subscribe to their own basic health insurance; otherwise they could be fined. Various private insurance companies offer this insurance, but the national government remains responsible for the overall accessibility and quality of the healthcare

system. These companies therefore have to offer a defined set of basic treatments, and they are not allowed to refuse healthcare or to impose special conditions. In 2015, Dutch residents spent an average of EUR 1 200 a year on basic healthcare insurance.

5.   The tasks of the GGD centres are specified by the national Public Health Act and generally include child healthcare, environmental health, socio-medical advice, periodic sanitary inspections, medical screening, epidemiology, health education and community mental health.

6.   This foundation has been supporting refugee students in the Netherlands since 1948. A small portion of funding comes from the municipality and is largely financed through private contributions and the national lottery. The foundation is moving from a model where it only supported students in obtaining a diploma to also facilitating refugees' access to the job market.

References

Arts, H. and A. Nabha (n.d.), *Humanity in Action*, https://www.humanityinaction.org/knowledgebase/6-education-in-the-netherlands-segregation-in-a-tolerant-society. [38]

Bakker, L., J. Dagevos and G. Engbersen (2013), "The importance of resources and security in the socio-economic integration of refugees. A study on the impact of length of stay in asylum accommodation and residence status on socio-economic integration for the four largest refugee groups in the NL", *Journal of International Migration and Integration*, pp. 431-448. [53]

Bruquetas-Callejo, M. et al. (2007), *Policymaking related to immigration and integration. The Dutch Case*, IMISCOE Working Paper: Country Report. [17]

Butter, E. (2009), *De zin en onzin van meinderhedenbeleid*, ACB Kenniscentrum online. [19]

CBS (2014), *Statistical Yearbook of the Netherlands*, Statistics Netherlands. [14]

CBS (2016), *Jaarrapport Integratie*, Centraal Bureau voor de Statistiek. [31]

CBS (2017), *Unemployment down among non-western migrant group*, https://www.cbs.nl/en-gb/news/2017/32/unemployment-down-among-non-western-migrant-group (accessed on 7 September 2017). [3]

Charbit, C. (2009), *Mind the gaps:managing mutual dependence in relations across levels of government*, OECD publisher. [10]

Charbit, C. (2011), *Governance of Public Policies in decentralised contexts:the multi-level apporach*, OECD publisher. [11]

Charbit, C. and O. Romano (2017), *Governing together: An international review of contracts across levels of government for regional development*, OECD Publishing. [6]

Charbit and Romano (forthcoming), *Governing together: an international review of contracts across levels of government for regional development*. [43]

Cities for local integration policy network (2010), *Intercultural policies and intergroup relations - Case study: Amsterdam, the Netherlands*, EUROFUND European Foundation for the Improvement of Living and Working Conditions. [30]

CLIP (2009), *Diversity policy in employment and service provision, case study: Amsterdam in the Netherlands*, European Foundation for the Improvement of Living and Working Conditions. [8]

de Graauw, E. and F. Vermeulen (2016), "Cities and th epolictics of immigrant integrtaion: a comparison of Berlin, Amsterdam, New York City and San Francisco", *Journal of Ethnic and MIgration Studies*, pp. 989-1012. [15]

Eurofund (2010), *Intercultural policies and intergroup relations - Case study: Amsterdam, the* [33]

Netherlands, European Foundation for the Improvement of Living and Working Conditions.

European Urban Knowledge Network (2012), *E-Libary*, http://www.eukn.eu/e-library/project/bericht/eventDetail/national-urban-policy-of-the-netherlands/ (accessed on 7 Septermber 2017). [45]

EUROSTAT (2016), *Record number of over 1.2 million first time asylum seekers registered in 2015.* [23]

eurostat (2016), *Urban Europe — statistics on cities, towns and suburbs*, eurostat. [47]

Geemente Amsterdam (2016b), *Vluchtelingenmonitor*, Gemeente Amsterdam. [9]

Gemeente Amsterdam (2015), *Beleidskader Vluchtelingen in Amsterdam*, Gemeente Amsterdam. [7]

Gemeente Amsterdam (2016a), *Begroeting*, Gemeente Amsterdam. [52]

Gemeente Amsterdam (n.d.), *Policy framework anti-discrimination Objetives 2015-2019*, Gemeente Amsterdam. [48]

Hamiltion, T. (2015), *theatlantic*, https://www.theatlantic.com/education/archive/2015/06/amsterdam-school-racial-segregation/396176/ (accessed on Septermber 2017). [37]

Hoekstra, M. (2014), *Baseline Study on Super-Diversiy and Urban Policies in Amsterdam*, Interethnic Coexistence in European Cities. [18]

HWWI (2007), *focus Migration country profiles*, Hamburg Institute of International Economics. [2]

Jaarboek Amsterdam (2016), *Amsterdam in cijfers.* [34]

Kennisplatform Integratie & Sammenleving (2016), *Diversiteit & Integratie: De Stand in Nederland*, Kennisplatform Integratie & Sammenleving. [54]

Kranendonk, M. et al. (2014), *Opkomst en stemgedrag van Amsterdammers met een migratie-achtergrond tijdens de gemeenteraadsverkiezingen van 19 maart 2014*, IMES Report. [16]

Maussen, M. (2009), *Constructing mosques : the governance of Islam in France and the Netherlands.* [20]

Ministerie van Sociale Zaken en Werkgelegenheid (2016), *Progess Report Participation Newcomers - to Dutch Parliament.* [46]

Musterd, S. (2016), *Changing welfare context and income segregation.* [35]

OECD/UCLG (2016), *Subnational Governments around the world: structure and finance*, OECD/UCLG. [40]

OECD (2006), *From immigration to integration: local solutions to a global challenge*, OECD Publishing. [29]

OECD (2010), *OECD Review of Migrant Education Netherlands*, OECD. [36]

OECD (2010), *Better Regulation in Europe: Netherlands*, OECD. [44]

OECD (2014), *OECD Territorial Reviews: Netherlands*, OECD. [42]

OECD (2016), *How's Life in the Netherlands*, OECD. [25]

OECD (2016), *Making Cities Work For All: Data And Actions For Inclusive Growth*, OECD [28]

Publisher.

OECD (2016a), *Recruiting Immigrant Workers: The Netherlands 2016*, OECD. [21]

OECD (2016b), *Making Integration Work*, OECD. [13]

OECD (2017), *The Governance of Land Use in the Netherlands: The Case of Amsterdam*, OECD Publishing. [27]

OECD (2017a), *International Migration Outlook*, OECD. [22]

OECD (2017b), *Multi-level governance reforms: Overview of the OECD Country Experiences*, OECD. [39]

OECD (2017b), *Subnational governments in OECD countries: Key data*, OECD. [50]

OECD (2017c), *OECD Regional Statistics*, OECD, http://dx.doi.org/10.1787/region-data-en. [41]

OECD (2018 Forthcoming), *Working together for integration of migrants and refugees at the local level*, OECD Publishing. [1]

OECD (forthcoming), *Working together for local integration of migrants and refugees*, OECD Publishing. [5]

OECD (forthcoming), *The Location of Asylum Seekers in OECD Regions and Cities*, OECD. [49]

OEDC Regional Well-Being (2016), *OECD Countries*, https://www.oecdregionalwellbeing.org/region.html#NL32 (accessed on September 2017). [26]

Scholten (2014), "Agenda Dynamics and the Multi-Level Governance of Migrant Integration. The Case of Dutch Migrant Integration Policies". [4]

Tammaru, T. et al. (2016), *Socio-Economic Segregation in European Capital Cities. East meets West*, Routhledge. [32]

UNHCR((n.d.)), *Resettlement Data finder*. [24]

UNSD (2017), *United Nations Statisctics Devision*, https://unstats.un.org/unsd/demographic/sconcerns/migration/migrmethods.htm#B (accessed on 2017). [12]

VNG (2014), *De wondere wereld van Gemeentefinancien 2014*, Vereniging van Nederlandse Gemeenten. [51]

Annex A. List of participants to the interviews with the OECD delegation 21-23 February 2017

	Name	Institution	Title
Ms.	Sabina Kekic	Municipality of Amsterdam	Advisor mayor of Amsterdam on European Affairs and refugees
Mr.	Jan van den Oord	Municipality of Amsterdam	Programme leader Participation, Language and Civic Integration (Programme Team Refugees)
Mr.	Niels Tubbing	Municipality of Amsterdam	Policy advisor Adult Education and Civic Integration
Mr.	Dimitris Grammatikas		EU migration specialist
Ms.	Agnieszka van den Bogaard	GGZ	Social worker
Mr.	Paul Mbikayi	Refugee Talent Hub	Managing Director of the Refugee Talent Hub
Ms.	Saskia Schoolland	COA	Location manager at COA
Mr.	Arjan Spit	Municipality of Amsterdam	Programme manager of the Housing Department
Mr.	Frans Heessels	Eigen werk, Municipality of Amsterdam	Team manager at *Eigen Werk Work Participation Income Department*
Ms.	Nienke van Dongen		Team coordinator at Implacement
Mr.	Albert de Voogd	UAF	Manager at UAF
Mr.	Martijn Kraaij	Ministry of SZW	National integration contact point at the Dutch Ministry of Social Affairs and Employment (SZW)
	Site Visit	Meevaart	
Ms.	Idske de Jong	Municipality of Amsterdam	Senior researcher
Ms.	Marjolein Martens	GGD	Regional coordinator for health issues concerning refugees
Mr.	Dirco Dekker	Manpower	Manager Social Development of Manpower
	Site Visit	Boost Ringdijk	
Mr.	Hans van Stee	Vluchtelingenwerk (Dutch Council for Refugees)	Manager at VluchtelingenWerk (local level)
Mr.	Henk Nijhuis	Vluchtelingenwerk (Dutch Council for Refugees)	Policy officer the Dutch Council for Refugees (national level)
Ms.	Anita Aleva	Municipality of Amsterdam	Senior policy advisor for the municipal districts
Mr.	Abdou Menebhi	EMCEMO (Morrocan migrant association)	Chairman

Annex B. Allocation of competences across levels of government related to migrant and refugee reception and integration

Policy area	National government	Province	Municipality
Asylum seekers and refugees	- Initial reception until status recognition via the Central Organ for Asylum Seekers (COA), which manages Dutch asylum seeker centres (AZCs) - Asylum application assessment and status recognition - Provision of allowance during asylum claim assessment (EUR 58/week) - Early integration package for recognised refugees (121 hours of Dutch classes and cultural background as well as coaching sessions) - Support for unaccompanied minors claiming asylum until 18 years old		- Provision of emergency shelter in co-operation with the COA - Establishment of regular AZCs in co-operation with the COA - Early integration opportunities such as studying, work or volunteer opportunities - Long-term integration: provide recognised refugees with housing and support for settling in - Responsibility for unaccompanied minors more than 18 years old - Organising language and integration courses for refugees in schools
Education	- Produce legislation (*Leerplichtwet*)		- Establishment and maintenance of primary and secondary education -Subsidize expenses of private primary schools in their areas - Supervision/ implementation of the Education Act (*Leerplichtwet*)
Language learning	- Set the conditions to pass the civic integration exam - Organisation of courses to pass the civic integration exam (Educational Department of the Ministry of Social Affairs) - Provide migrants and refugees with grants for language classes		- Provides additional courses to the groups who don't have to pass the Civic Integration Exam
Vocational training policy			- Establishment and maintenance of schools - Adult education (programming and financing)
Social policy	- The national unemployment agency (UWV) sets the criteria for the allocation of social welfare		- Social assistance: social welfare, welfare payments, social services administration – Elderly and child care – Social integration of people with

Policy area	National government	Province	Municipality
			disabilities
			– Social integration of foreigners
			- Youth policy: financing youth organisations; youth and child protection; youth probation and youth care
			-Youth assistance and welfare services
Employment	- The UWV allocates unemployment benefits and other reintegration measures through regional labour market offices (central government agencies) The Ministry of Social Affairs and Employment organises roundtables with relevant stakeholders to set guidelines on key employment issues concerning migrant integration (e.g. youth, discrimination)	- Functional regional boards for employment services - In charge of dialogue for co-operation between the public authorities and business	- Local social assistance and employment schemes – Local measures for access to and participation in the labour market – Back to work programme: reintegration into the labour market, including for young disabled (tasks decentralised in the 2015 reform – *cf.* Participation Act) – Training and encouraging entrepreneurship (e.g. *Eigen Werk*)
Housing	- Provides funding for building social housing but is accessible through sometimes very restrictive tenders	- Allocation of quota (social housing) and municipal subsidies	- Building and management of social housing and municipal land, in collaboration with housing associations (six in the city of Amsterdam)
Spatial planning		- Drawing up regional plans – Endorsement of municipal land-use plans	- Drawing up land-use plans - Planning permissions - Urban planning, development and regeneration
Public health	- Responsible for regional healthcare services (a central government agency)		- Public health and hygiene department (GGD) - Municipal medical services (e.g. vaccination, disease prevention) – Elderly and youth healthcare – Long-term care
Public administration		- Supervision of municipal finance and regional water authorities	- Administrative services (marriage, birth, etc.)
Public order and Safety	- Responsible for public defence and justice - Regional police services		- Public order in the municipality and relationships with police forces – Crime prevention – Public safety
Economic development	- National economic development	- Regional economic development – Agriculture and rural development Partnership between public authorities and	– Local economic development

Policy area	National government	Province	Municipality
		businesses	
		– Regional marketing to attract business	
		– Stimulation of entrepreneurship	

Source: Findings from OECD mission to Amsterdam (21-23 February 2017) and OECD (2014), *OECD Territorial Reviews: Netherlands 2014*, http://dx.doi.org/10.1787/9789264209527-en.

ORGANISATION FOR ECONOMIC CO-OPERATION AND DEVELOPMENT

The OECD is a unique forum where governments work together to address the economic, social and environmental challenges of globalisation. The OECD is also at the forefront of efforts to understand and to help governments respond to new developments and concerns, such as corporate governance, the information economy and the challenges of an ageing population. The Organisation provides a setting where governments can compare policy experiences, seek answers to common problems, identify good practice and work to co-ordinate domestic and international policies.

The OECD member countries are: Australia, Austria, Belgium, Canada, Chile, the Czech Republic, Denmark, Estonia, Finland, France, Germany, Greece, Hungary, Iceland, Ireland, Israel, Italy, Japan, Korea, Latvia, Luxembourg, Mexico, the Netherlands, New Zealand, Norway, Poland, Portugal, the Slovak Republic, Slovenia, Spain, Sweden, Switzerland, Turkey, the United Kingdom and the United States. The European Union takes part in the work of the OECD.

OECD Publishing disseminates widely the results of the Organisation's statistics gathering and research on economic, social and environmental issues, as well as the conventions, guidelines and standards agreed by its members.

OECD PUBLISHING, 2, rue André-Pascal, 75775 PARIS CEDEX 16
(85 2018 10 1 P) ISBN 978-92-64-29971-9 – 2018